Hay '91

+ from Charles Macleod +
Jan
Dec 1991
cat 12.91

DESIGNING PLACES FOR PEOPLE

DESIGNING PLACES FOR PEOPLE

A Handbook on Human Behavior for Architects, Designers, and Facility Managers

by C.M. Deasy, FAIA
in collaboration with
Thomas E. Lasswell, Ph.D.

WHITNEY LIBRARY OF DESIGN
an imprint of Watson-Guptill Publications/New York

Copyright © 1985 by C. M. Deasy and Thomas E. Lasswell

First published 1985 in New York by the Whitney Library of Design,
an imprint of Watson-Guptill Publications,
a division of Billboard Publications, Inc.,
1515 Broadway, New York, N.Y. 10036

Library of Congress Cataloging in Publication Data
Deasy, C. M.
  Designing places for people.
  Includes index.
  1. Architecture—Human factors. 2. Architecture—
Environmental aspects. I. Lasswell, Thomas E. II. Title.
NA2542.4.D4   1985   720′.1′03   85-3145
ISBN 0-8230-7152-9

Distributed in the United Kingdom by Phaidon Press Ltd.,
Littlegate House, St. Ebbe's St., Oxford

Manufactured in U.S.A.

First printing, 1985

1 2 3 4 5 6 7 8 9 / 90 89 88 87 86 85

FOREWORD

I have always been amused by the photographs that architects take of their buildings. They are invariably very artistic in intent and execution but do not include any people. A building, no matter how well it may be designed, cannot be successful without people, and particularly people who are enjoying themselves.

Why is one restaurant more successful than another when both have similar menu fare? Obviously it has to do with the ambience of the space and the warmth with which the guests were greeted when they arrived.

Many times I have viewed similar buildings or spaces, the first devoid of people and the second bubbling with activity. Why?

It is a criticism leveled at many architects and designers that they do not consider down-to-earth human frailties and desires when creating spaces for human habitation. These professions must develop and encourage people who are, to a much larger degree, "observers"—absorbing what people do and do not like. Certainly one of the greatest human games is "people-watching."

In short, does the human feel good in a particular space? To this end, the subject of this text is of great interest to me and should be to all architects and designers of "places for people." Presenting the human behavioral issues to those directly responsible for the architectural side of developing the world around us and in a language specifically geared to these professionals, as this text does, helps fill a surprising void of information available in this field. Information that can and should be used by designers every day in their work.

As Mr. Deasy points out in his opening, the nature of our buildings and streets affects our behavior, affects the way we feel about ourselves and, importantly, how we get along with others.

That is a uniquely significant responsibility in today's society and one that our architects, designers, and planners cannot take lightly.

The material in this text is highly useful. The subject, presentation, and information presented here portray an idea whose time has come.

MacDonald G. Becket, FAIA
The Becket Group

CONTENTS

PREFACE

During years of architectural practice spent in designing buildings that were responsive to both the needs and the feelings of the people who used them, I collected a great deal of information about the ways human behavior is influenced by the buildings humans inhabit. Much of this information was derived from research done in connection with specific architectural design projects. More of it was drawn from sources in the human sciences and from the emerging field of environmental design research.

Some of this material has been discussed in magazine articles, in a series of privately printed monographs, and in an earlier book, *Design for Human Affairs*. None of it, however, has ever been collected and arranged for simple and easy use by working designers. This handbook, *Designing Places for People*, will, I hope, serve that need.

The task of sorting through the information available and translating it into design recommendations has been long and complicated. Fortunately, I have had expert help from a variety of sources. The collaboration of Dr. Thomas Lasswell, Professor of Sociology at the University of Southern California, has been especially important in the preparation of this text as it has been for many years in connection with many other projects. Stephen Kliment, FAIA, Executive Editor of the Whitney Library of Design, has been patiently helpful over a long gestation and demonstrated an unusual grasp of some esoteric subject matter. Susan Davis, developmental editor, and Brooke Dramer, associate editor, have polished both the ideas and the syntax to make the pages that follow clearer and more readable. I must also give thanks for the assistance provided by the National Endowment for the Arts in the form of Grant R81-42-10N.

This book is a useful, practical resource for the designers as well as the operators and managers of buildings and public places. As the first handbook of this type it will, in time, be expanded and improved. It is my hope that readers from all the fields that are concerned with behavior and environment will send me their comments and suggestions. These pages can then serve as a channel of communication between the research fraternity and those who design and administer the places where people live and interact. This will benefit all of us who share a concern for improving the design process. More important, it will greatly benefit the general public.

Such a result would be a rich reward for the time and effort that have gone into the preparation of this book.

C. M. DEASY, FAIA

1 HUMAN BEHAVIOR AND THE DESIGNER

Although the design professions work with different materials and employ different techniques to solve their problems, they share their only client—the human race—in common. Architects, landscape architects, interior designers, graphic designers, industrial designers, urban designers, and other professionals in the expanding field of environmental design accept without question the fundamental assumption that their work is designed for, and must be useful to, human beings.

In the process of creating buildings, landscapes, and cityscapes these same professionals must, of course, deal with serious problems of technology, health and safety, legal constraints, and economics. Fortunately they have available to them a wealth of guides, handbooks, building codes, and estimating manuals that summarize this needed information in concise and convenient form. If they need to know the length of a football field, the size of a hospital bed, or the turning radius of a truck and trailer, this information has also been collected and codified to expedite the design process. As far as products and processes are concerned, the design professions work with an excellent information base.

In view of the excellent information available on products and processes, it is surprising to find that there is so little information available to designers about their principal concern, the human client. There are, to be sure, excellent reference works on anthropometry, the study of the human body and its functional capabilities. As a result designers have at hand data on the physical dimensions of human beings in every conceivable posture: reclining, sitting, kneeling, standing, sleeping, and awake. In the critical matter of the *behavioral dimensions* of human beings, however, the situation is different. In spite of the enormous body of research done within the human sciences on the human species and the growing volume of studies focused specifically on the relationship between environment and behavior, none of this information has been summarized in a form that can be used readily by designers and that fits naturally into the design process.

This is an unfortunate void. The nature of the buildings and streets of the cities where we live affects our behavior, the way we feel about ourselves, and most important, the way we get along with others. If designers were able to work with a clear understanding of the relationships between behavior and environment, they could create communities where these effects are positive and beneficial. Without such an understanding, the behavioral effects of design are haphazard at best and disastrous at worst. It is like flying without a map or compass. Behavior will be affected in any case, but it may be in ways that were never intended or never even imagined. It seems ironic that the professionals who have the principal responsibility for designing the places where humans live, work, and play should not have access to information that is so important to the people for whom they design.

ENVIRONMENT INFLUENCES BEHAVIOR

The ways in which the design of the human environment affects human behavior are not trivial. One easily understood aspect is the matter of cooperation. Much of modern life depends on cooperation between individuals—on the streets, in the neighborhood, and especially in the workplace. Community living would be much less tolerable if people generally did not cooperate in waiting for pedestrians to clear the crosswalk, holding the door for people with bundles, answering the telephone for the person at the next desk, or accepting deliveries for the next-door neighbor. If the design of these places embodies the characteristics that make cooperation easy and convenient, then people can function more effectively and everyone is better off. If these characteristics are not present, then people will be subject to unnecessary friction and conflict.

Cooperation is only one of a number of equally important considerations. Making friends with others is an important matter for most people. So is the feeling of personal worthiness. Both of these concerns are directly affected by our environment. If the apartment stairs and walks are arranged so that we meet our neighbors occasionally, we might find that we like them. If the walks and stairs are arranged so that we never meet, we will never know whether we like them or not. In a similar way, our sense of our own worth is influenced by the accommodations that are provided for us when we do business with others. If the doctors, merchants, and bankers we do business with want us to come back, they must demonstrate that they regard us as important.

There are other equally down-to-earth ways in which the environment relates to our behavior. Communicating with others in order to share our experiences and find out what is going on is another matter that is very important to most people. So is the problem of wayfinding. The ease and accuracy with which we both communicate and find our way through the urban landscape is largely contingent on the nature of the surrounding environment. Everyone has a favorite horror story about the meeting or conference that failed because it was impossible to see or to hear. We have also experienced some frustration in trying to find someplace or someone in a building complex without signs or markings. Any environment that is inadequate for its intended purpose, that frustrates and annoys us, or that limits our ability to accomplish our purposes has a direct bearing on human behavior. From finding friends to finding our way, these are all matters that are of great importance to human beings. For any designer to ignore them would be to ignore what human beings are all about.

UTILIZING BEHAVIORAL RESEARCH

Anyone who has made a serious effort to search through the research literature of the human sciences for information that can be directly applied in the design process will have no trouble understanding why it is not easily available. One reason is that there is so much of it. The amount of study devoted to the human species is awesome, and the flood of new information shows no sign of letting up. Another is that seldom is it related obviously and clearly to a designer's information needs. A sociological study on the subject of distributive justice might not appear to have much to do with the layout of office spaces and the kind of equipment and furnishings that are supplied, but the two are directly related. This is the kind of information office planners need to know about. When they allocate space, furnishings, and equipment, they are at the same time allocating status, and any unjust allocations will surely annoy individuals who get less than their peers. Unfortunately, as long as these data are filed under the heading "distributive justice," it is unlikely that they will be widely available to designers. As a result there is a two-fold need: Useful information must be located, and it must be translated from the terminology of the human sciences to the language of design.

There is yet another problem that must be dealt with in compiling useful information for designers: It is that some findings in the field of the human sciences, though they may have important implications about the environment, have not been replicated and are not universally accepted as representing soundly based principles. As a consequence the information covered in the following chapters has been selected to meet certain criteria:

- It is based on a list of human characteristics that is accepted widely in the fields of sociology and psychology.
- Only those characteristics that have a clear relationship to the designed environment have been used in developing recommendations.
- Recommendations are not made in the abstract. They are related to a wide range of actual design problems.
- The recommendations are expressed in the terminology of the design field.

These criteria have been adopted to ensure that the material in the book will be clearly and directly useful to environmental designers in the form they need. The book does not deal with global generalities and is not a general compendium on the subject of human behavior. It deals only with those matters where there is a clear relationship between environment and behavior, between the surroundings in which we live and work and the way we feel and act. These are the factors that create the almost imperceptible differences that make one location enjoyable and productive and another intolerable.

It is not unreasonable to wonder why, if environment and behavior are closely related, there is not more obvious outcry against the kind of planning that puts people in stressful situations. One explanation, as some designers have noted ruefully, is that people do not always accept meekly what is given to them. They will blithely make hash out of the designer's best ideas as they convert their offices, apartments, or dormitory rooms into something better suited to their purposes. Another reason is that the human species is remarkably adaptable. It is, in fact, unique in its ability to adapt to every living zone on this planet. This same adaptability makes it possible for people to function, and to function well, under circumstances that they would never choose if they were offered any alternatives. This universal adaptability is hardly an excuse for careless planning. If the design professions seriously accept a commitment to make life better for their human clients, they cannot avoid the responsibility of creating situations where these clients perform at their best *because* of their environment rather than in spite of it.

HUMAN NATURE CANNOT BE PREDICTED INTUITIVELY

There is one last question about human behavior that must be dealt with. It concerns the point of view that argues that it is hardly necessary for designers to be concerned with the study of human nature since they are, of necessity, humans themselves and therefore know how humans react. This is not a tenable point of view. Several careful studies have shown that by the time designers have gone through their rigorous training, their attitudes and values concerning design questions are strikingly at variance with the general public. A more important consideration is that, in spite of what common sense might suggest, human behavior cannot be predicted intuitively; in fact, it is sometimes counter intuitive. It is not uncommon to find, for instance, that when noisy office equipment is quieted, complaints about noise increase because it is now possible to hear people talking on the telephone. Equipment noise can be annoying, but conversations are more distracting because we are curious about what other people are saying.

This sequence of photographs shows that, while both doors function perfectly, entering traffic elects to use the left-hand door instead of "passing to the right." As the last picture indicates, people exiting the building use what is for them the right-hand door, resulting in a series of collisions at the entrance.

Even our faith in universally accepted custom may be ill founded. It is a generally accepted concept in North America that traffic moves to the right; roadways, sidewalks, and building entrances are predicated on that assumption. Careful observation of what actually happens, however, indicates that such is not necessarily the case. While a healthy respect for the lethal consequences of being unique keeps vehicular traffic moving to the right, that is not true elsewhere. One consequence is that traffic at building entrances is often unnecessarily jammed up because the traffic streams have not been clearly separated. The accompanying photos were taken at a branch library and show that while both doors were functioning perfectly and there was no obvious reason for their choice, the people entering the building consistently entered through the lefthand door. The people exiting the building, however, consistently used what was for them the righthand door. The result was a series of headon collisions. While this is not a major problem, it illustrates an important point. The architect who designed the entrance surely had no intention of causing this inconvenience. The problem could easily have been avoided by separating the two doors into an entrance and an exit. Unfortunately, neither this nor any other problem can be solved unless its existence is recognized. As long as we make "assumptions" about human behavior rather than finding out about it, we are likely to continue to make similar errors.

This book is dedicated to the following premises:

- The principal reason for building anything is to help people accomplish their purposes as effectively as possible.
- Human effectiveness in any activity is greatly influenced by social and psychological factors.
- Environmental designers should use the knowledge of human behavior to create places that help people accomplish their purposes with a maximum of satisfaction and a minimum of friction and frustration.

The following chapters have been prepared to help designers meet this commitment. There is an additional benefit that may not be apparent immediately. A better understanding of the interrelationship between environment and behavior is a spur to creativity. The concerns that are dealt with in this book will complicate a designer's work to some degree but at the same time they offer an opportunity to create new and more effective solutions to old problems. Most designers would consider that a fair trade.

2 USING BEHAVIORAL SCIENCE IN THE DESIGN PROCESS

When designers are involved in developing the solution to a design problem, they utilize information in two forms. They work fastest with information that they have in their memories. If the problem is new to them, however, they turn to reference sources or special consultants for the specific data that may be needed. An experienced architect might know a great deal about bank layout and operation, but if he or she had never dealt with automated teller installations before, some accurate and reliable information would be sought from outside sources to ensure that the installation is properly designed.

Another characteristic of the design process is that in practice, it is conducted under considerable time pressure. A designer may not realize that certain information is needed until the process is well advanced. At that point there is little time for leisurely research; the necessary information must be located and used as quickly as possible. There is a temptation at this point to "guess" at the answers, but this must be avoided at all costs. In the design world, mistakes last a long time and the penalties for wrong guesses can be very punishing.

The information in the following chapters is arranged to fit into the process described above. Chapter 3, *The Nature of Human Nature,* contains background information on human behavior that should help designers understand the underlying relationships between environment and behavior. This is material that should be studied and reflected on as part of any individual's general fund of knowledge.

Chapters 4 through 11 deal with specific places where people live together, work together, meet together, shop together, and learn together. Information about these places is briefly summarized, and recommendations are made to assist the designer in resolving those aspects of the problem that deal with human behavior. Photographs and diagrams are used to illustrate the points made in the text, but it should be understood that these are not intended to dictate solutions. In most instances a number of satisfactory solutions can be worked out that all embody the principles illustrated. A designer working on a shopping complex or furnishing a hospital lobby can turn directly to a chapter that discusses these places and find information that relates specifically to these problems. Obviously this information will mean more and can be used with greater effect by someone who has taken the time to study Chapter 3.

A last resource is contained in the Bibliography list at the end of the book. There is a wealth of detailed data available to the designer that can and should be used to supplement the basic concepts discussed in this book. It does not deal uniformly with all aspects of environment, however. As is true in most fields, research follows funding and funding follows the national preoccupation. As a result such subjects as health care and public safety receive considerably more attention than apartment planning or park layout. Nonetheless, the bibliography is a rich lode that should be carefully mined.

CONSTRUCTING A BEHAVIORAL PROGRAM

The ideal time to use this information is in the *predesign* or *programming* stage. Designers are very familiar with the list of requirements supplied by the client and called the *program* or the *brief*. These documents vary greatly in quality and detail. Sometimes they are expertly prepared by professional programming firms and sometimes they are actually written on the proverbial "back of a napkin." In some instances informal programs are prepared by the designer who, lacking any other guidance, feels the need for establishing goals and criteria as an aid in defining the project. Whatever the source of the program, it will seldom spell out the precise behavioral consequences that should be sought or how they are to be achieved. It is not unusual to find a preamble that stresses the need for "warm and sympathetic environment" or "an environment that will involve the users," but it is notoriously difficult to translate such generalizations into design specifics.

When the program is received, it should be reviewed and annotated or supplemented with human behavior goals. A specific document should be prepared that goes through each segment of the building program and stipulates precisely defined goals. A behavioral supplement is not a place for vague generalities. It should be as precise in its own way as the building program itself. It is not essential that this supplement be done by the designer. It could also be done by the individual who prepares the program. Experience indicates, however, that the chances of these goals being implemented and actually being reflected in the finished solution are much better if the designer who works on the project is involved in the process of defining the goals.

A brief example can illustrate how this would be done. The program or list of required facilities for the design of a secondary school would surely specify a site and would require a variety of special spaces such as an office, classrooms, an assembly room, a cafeteria, and a teachers lounge. Each one of these spaces represents a different set of functional requirements as well as a different set of social and psychological relationships. In developing a list of specific behavioral suggestions for each aspect of this project, the designer would consult whichever of the following chapters deals with the underlying relationships between the people involved. Chapter 8, *Learning Together*, would be an obvious source. It not only covers classrooms and lecture halls in general but also discusses the layout of the school grounds. Chapter 5, *Working Together*, discusses problems that are common in both private and shared office spaces in schools or other institutions.

The source of information about other spaces may not be so obvious at first. It is necessary to think in terms of the social nature of the activity that occurs in the space. Assembly rooms and teachers lounges are vastly different places, yet both share a similar purpose: They are places where people meet together. Recommendations about such places will be found in Chapter 6, *Meeting Together*. School cafeterias and faculty dining rooms are not mentioned in the text, but the important social aspects of eating together are discussed under the heading of "A Place to Eat" in Chapter 7.

This is by no means the end of the search. Every school will have some waiting area for the public, whether it is spelled out in the program or not. Useful information on this subject will be found in Chapter 10, *Public Spaces–Inside*. Since every public school ground is to some degree a neighborhood amenity, the recommendations in Chapter 11, *Public Spaces–Outside*, may contribute something to the design of the outside areas of the school. In addition, every school must communicate its identity and purpose to the public through signs of some kind and provide an understandable organization so that newcomers can find their way around. The discussion in Chapter 3 on "Communications" and "Wayfinding" offers some helpful information on dealing with these problems.

This is the process by which information on human behavior is assembled and incorporated into the design process. It does not deal in broad generalities at all. There are no single heroic solutions. No single bit of information is likely to make an earthshaking difference in the end product. All the bits and pieces add up, however. The cumulative effect is to create an institution or an environment that makes it possible for people to achieve their goals with a minimum of frustration and a maximum of satisfaction. This is not the same as saying that everyone will live happily ever after. There are too many factors, other than our immediate surroundings, that affect our general well-being. All that is implied here is that, so far as the environment affects us, the positive, supportive aspects will be emphasized and the frustrating, negative aspects will be minimized. No one should underestimate that accomplishment. It represents an enormous step forward in the field of environmental design.

It would be inaccurate to assume that, by using the information in this handbook, all the aspects of human behavior that might be important in any given project will be covered. As a handbook, it deals with principles that apply to a wide spectrum of design projects and the conditions that are normally encountered in North America. It does not pretend to cover all situations everywhere. There will be instances where the unique nature of the project, its size and scale, or the number of people involved will make it desirable, or even imperative, to conduct specific research on the groups of people who will be affected. The human sciences have developed a variety of research techniques for gathering information that can be very valuable to the design professions. They are practical, effective, and have been very productive in providing answers to some perplexing design problems.

One approach to problems of this nature is to construct a careful behavioral program, or supplement to the building program, based on the information in this handbook. It should then be possible to determine if major questions or uncertainties remain that require further research. Before embarking on such activities, it would be wise to consult some of the books that deal specifically with the problem of employing behavior research techniques in the design field.

Even if there are no unanswered questions that would warrant a special research program, it may be justified for other reasons. There is one benefit resulting from direct research in this field that is too often overlooked. People like to feel that they have some degree of control over their lives and some voice in their destiny. As a consequence, involving the people who will be affected by any design project in the decision-making process through survey research techniques, observations, or interviews can be very beneficial. These benefits will derive in part from the fact that the designer has better, more relevant information about the problem. Even more important, however, is the fact that the users who have been involved will be predisposed to like what they get and to want it to work.

3 THE NATURE OF HUMAN NATURE

Human behavior is a complex subject. It is the focus of a whole family of scientific disciplines. It has drawn the attention of outstanding scholars and researchers in the fields of psychology, sociology, and anthropology. It has intrigued poets, playwrights, and philosophers through the ages and formed the basis for our culture's greatest literary masterpieces. The amount of published information on human behavior is enough to dismay even the most dedicated investigator.

Fortunately, as far as designers are concerned, only a limited portion of this information deals with the relationship between behavior and environment. While a broad understanding of human nature is an invaluable asset to anyone, and further reading of the excellent sources listed in the selected Bibliography is strongly recommended, this book makes no attempt to cover the subject completely. It is focused specifically on those aspects of human behavior that are clearly related to the design field, especially the fields of architecture, interior design, furniture design, landscape architecture, and urban design.

While human interaction is complex, it is rooted in a limited number of motivating factors. Different authorities offer different lists of these essential factors but they do not vary in serious ways. Alexander Leighton has proposed a list of 10 "essential striving sentiments" ranging from *Physical Security* to *A Sense of Belonging to a Moral Order*. Abraham Maslow has condensed his hierarchy into four elements:

- Food and Drink Needs
- Security and Safety Needs
- The Need for Affection
- The Need for Self-Actualization

Regardless of the length of the list, there are certain aspects that are constant. Not all of these motivating factors are of equal importance, nor do they have the same priority at all stages of life. If the imperative needs for food and drink become difficult to satisfy, there will be little concern for such abstract matters as self-actualization. In societies where food and security are more or less assured, however, the needs for affection and self-actualization become much more important.

The same change in priorities occurs with age. Young adults are less concerned with security than their elders but are much concerned with winning the affection and esteem of their own age group.

The recommendations made in this book are derived from a subset of motivating factors that are in some way affected by the environment and can be influenced by designers who work in environmental fields. They are:

Friendship Formation

Group Membership

Personal Space

Personal Status

Territoriality

Communications

Cue Searching

Personal Safety

This list may seem to imply that a designer is not only capable of making a positive impact on many lives but also bears some responsibility for how they turn out. No such implication is intended. There is no magic available to a designer that can cause two strangers to become friends or that will open membership in a warm and supportive group to someone who is alone. A designer's responsibility is to provide settings that encourage the interactions that lead to friendship and, perhaps more important, to avoid the creation of settings that discourage or prevent such interactions. That, however, is an important responsibility.

Because the motivating factors are listed above as discrete items and are each treated separately in the following text, it may appear that each deals with a distinct and separate aspect of human nature. That creates an erroneous impression. In fact, all aspects of human nature are so interrelated that the boundaries between them are difficult to establish. While it is convenient to discuss friendship formation and the urge to seek group membership as separate matters, the two are closely related. It would be equally hard to draw a line between an individual's concern about personal status and territorial feelings about personal rights. It is more accurate to view human beings as subject to a spectrum of motivating factors—some innate, some culturally based. Whatever the source, these factors interact in different ways at different times to form that phenomenon we call human nature.

Subsequent chapters deal with the design of places where people live and work. In each instance the motivating factors that are likely to be most important in those places are analyzed and recommendations made about design features. Thus, it is possible to go directly to the section on schools or apartment houses for information without reading this general discussion about the factors with which a designer is supposed to be concerned. It would be much more productive, however, to study the following material carefully. These factors are the foundation on which all the recommendations that follow are made. A thorough understanding of them will not only make the detailed recommendations more easily understood; it will enable the designer to make intelligent projections about new situations and different projects that are not covered in this book.

FRIENDSHIP FORMATION

Friendships are formed on the basis of shared interests and backgrounds. As interests, hobbies, family, or careers change, people become open to new friendships. The friendships that are then formed are largely affected by opportunity. People make friends from contacts at school, at work, in their neighborhoods, and at clubs and social gatherings. Contact is an indispensable part of the process.

Studies made in offices, apartment complexes, college dormitories, and housing for the elderly repeatedly demonstrate the importance of proximity in initiating social contact. People select friends from the groups they know, and the groups they know best are those closest to them. It is surprising how much influence even small distances can have on this process. Research in an English study (as reported by Peter Manning) indicated that when office workers were asked to list their friends, 39% of the names on the list were of people who worked within 12 feet. The percentage dropped as the distance increased. Only 11% of the names on the list were people who worked at a distance of 36 feet.

Friendships formed through contacts made as a result of living close together have a tendency to persist as long as the shared interests persist. In a dormitory study conducted at Princeton by F. Duncan Case, 90% of sophomore dormitory residents were found to select their roommates from among the group they knew in their freshman dorms. This effect was so strong that even by their senior years 86% chose roommates they had met in their freshman dorms.

In understanding the effect of closeness on social contact, it is necessary to recognize that it is functional rather than physical distance that makes the difference. People may live just inches apart, separated only by a wall, but if they use different stairs, travel different paths, or follow different schedules, they may never even see each other. Even in a business office, if some employees in one department use a different exit or a different corridor from the other employees, they may have very little direct contact. Physical closeness is important, but where people meet is determined by the configuration of buildings and their grounds, the location of exits, stairways, parking lots, staff cafeterias, elevators, playgrounds, laundry rooms, and all the other facilities that cause people to move in specific paths.

Left: Centrifugal effect. *Adjacent tenants are isolated by the stair locations.*
Right: Centripetal effect. *Adjacent tenants are brought into contact by the stair locations.*

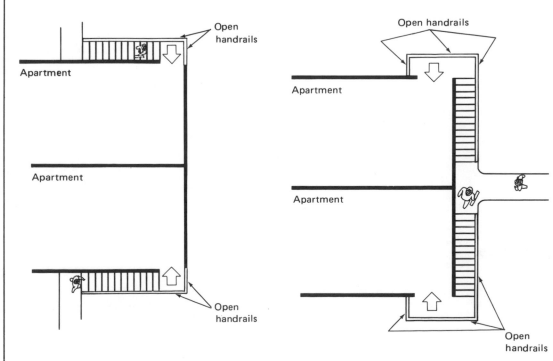

It is easy to see why designers share some responsibility for social interaction. They create the conditions that determine which paths people will follow and, as a consequence, where they will meet. F. Duncan Case refers to these as "architecturally determined domains of acquaintance." These domains of acquaintance occur in buildings whether they are intended or not. The building plan may tend to disperse people in a centrifugal fashion that minimizes contact, or it may bring them together in a centripetal fashion that increases contact without anyone ever having considered the benefits or drawbacks of either effect. There are times when either one of these effects might be desirable, so it is important to design with a clear understanding of how a plan affects friendship formation.

GROUP MEMBERSHIP

Being or not being a member of a definite social group is one part of the way people define themselves and is thus a matter of importance to most people. It is an extension of our need to form friendships and a mark of the social nature of humankind. Friendship groups are usually quite small. While an individual may be a member of a social club or fraternity with an extensive membership and may be familiar with all the members, that individual would not necessarily regard them all as close friends.

The tendency to affiliate with small groups is marked. The general rules for appropriate behavior can be more easily comprehended in small groups where communications are easier and more accurate. The small group also offers each member a better opportunity to participate in group discussions and decisions.

Studies made of informal groups observed in public places show that 71% contained only two individuals, 21% three individuals, 6% four individuals, and only 2% five or more individuals. This suggests that seating arrangements in parks, hotel lobbies, and other public gathering places should be designed with such small groups in mind. These small groups may have met or come together in some preferred gathering spot or social center such as the game area in the park, the snack bar on the college campus, the bar at the country club, a favored beach, or the neighborhood tavern. In such places there may be a good deal of movement between groups. As newcomers join a group and swell its numbers, some members will split off and form a new group. This kind of action is commonplace at cocktail parties, receptions, and similar social gatherings.

The human tendency to form groups suggests the need for places where groups can form. Lounges, lobbies, and recreation rooms are obvious examples of spaces that accommodate this need. It is doubtful, though, that such specifically designated facilities take care of all the needs. Social groups tend to form wherever people of like interest come in contact with one another in public corridors, stairways, laundry rooms, parks, and bus stops. If a designer can reasonably infer where trafficways will intersect or where people will be drawn by necessity, it can be assumed that groups will form at these points and should probably be provided with seating and other conveniences.

PERSONAL SPACE

People in our society have strong feelings about controlling access to their persons. These feelings manifest themselves in several ways. They have a pronounced effect on the spacing or separation that people elect when dealing with other people. They are also the basis for the widely held preferences for private, personal spaces at home and at work.

The feeling about personal space that is common in North America is not necessarily a universal emotion. Other societies have different feelings about pri-

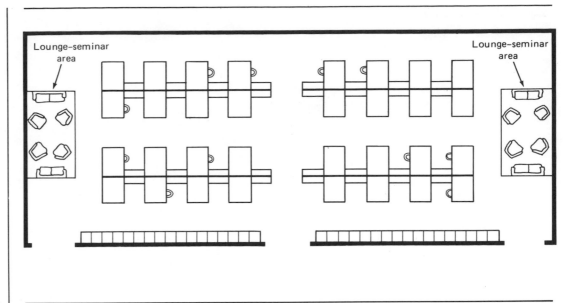

Centrifugal effect. *The location of the seminar areas in this design laboratory tends to keep the two class sections apart.*

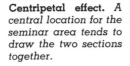

Centripetal effect. *A central location for the seminar area tends to draw the two sections together.*

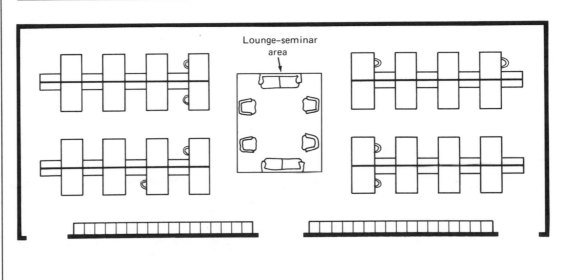

vacy and physical contact. In some, privacy is almost nonexistent; even strangers will converse, negotiate, or argue at close ranges that would make many people in our society exceedingly uncomfortable. Since North America has been populated by people with many different cultural backgrounds that instill different feelings about personal space, our reactions are not uniform. They are, however, consistent enough to provide useful guidelines for designers.

Anthropologist Edward T. Hall has described a series of distances that are normally used by people in North America in relating to others: intimate distance, personal distance, social distance, and public distance.

INTIMATE DISTANCE

This ranges from actual contact to a distance of 18 inches. It is reserved for lovers, family, small children, or very close friends. Many American adults would not feel at ease at such close range in public places. The common exception to this general rule is when people are forced into close quarters, as when riding in an elevator or on a bus or subway. Under these circumstances they tend to "cocoon," or wrap an invisible mantle of protection around themselves for the duration of the contact.

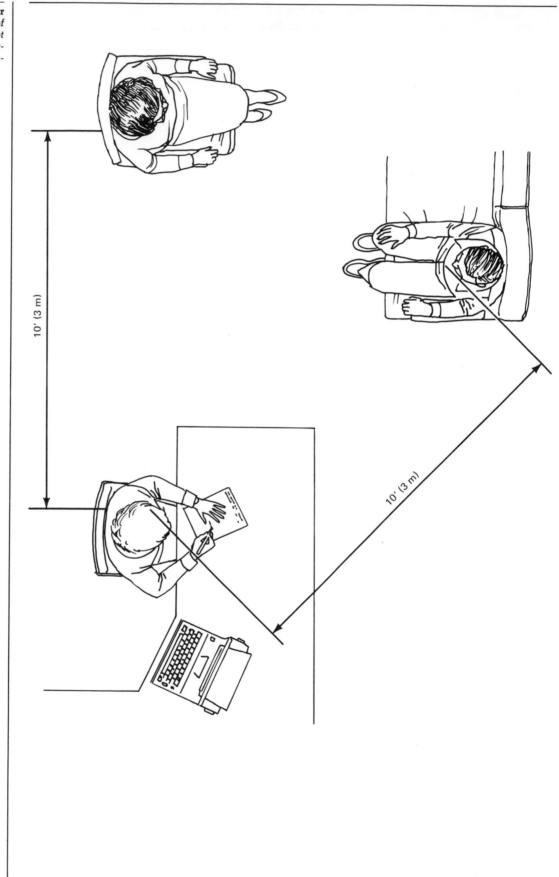

Social distance—far phase. *At a distance of about 10 feet, it is not considered rude to ignore a visitor and continue working.*

10' (3 m)

10' (3 m)

PERSONAL DISTANCE

Ranges from one and one-half to four feet. These numbers roughly define the bubble of "Personal Space" that surrounds most people. This is a protected area, where strangers would not be welcome. At its farther limit it holds other people "at arms length."

SOCIAL DISTANCE

From four to twelve feet. This is the range in which most public interactions are observed in America. As a result, it is a range that is of special interest to designers.

The closer part of the social distance range, from 4 to 7 feet, is a normal spacing for people who work together. It is also customary at social gatherings (assuming there is enough room to permit such distances). At such distances, speech and expressions are clear and communications are highly efficient and accurate. In arranging seating in public places it is important that, when people are seated, their heads are within this range or can be shifted to fall within this range.

The farther part of the range, from 7 to 12 feet, is more formal, is more likely to be used with strangers, and is used frequently when a subordinate is talking to "the boss." Private offices are sometimes arranged to hold visitors at this distance. If the office occupant elects a less formal distance, a move can be made to an alternate seating arrangement that permits closer spacing.

Social distance, as the term is used by Edward Hall, embraces a dimension that is uniquely important to designers. Starting at about 10 feet it is not considered rude to ignore a visitor and continue working. A receptionist, for example, can feel free to go ahead with other work if office visitors are seated 10 or more feet from the reception desk. This is especially true if they are not seated directly in front of the receptionist but are off to one side.

PUBLIC DISTANCE

From 12 to 25 feet. This is the range where noninvolvement begins. It is possible to pass someone you know within this distance without having to stop and exchange greetings. If designers wanted to make that option, *noninvolvement,* available, they would have to provide entrances and walkways over 12 feet wide. The far edge of public distance is the distance preserved around important public figures.

PROXEMICS

The distancing aspect of personal space, called *proxemics,* is an important concern in environmental design. It is well worth further study by anyone working in this field.

There are some modifications of the general rules cited above that affect the planning and design fields. While it would be considered a rude invasion if a stranger walked up to within a foot or two of your face, clearly penetrating your bubble of personal space, someone moving that close to your side (as might happen on the sidewalk) or standing behind you (as might happen in a queue) would not be bothersome unless that person attempted to touch you. The personal-space bubble is not an invisible circle with you at the center. It encloses more space in front of you than in back.

There are many applications of proxemics in the design field. Among other things, it indicates the necessity of adequate spacing between all fixtures in public toilets, or the use of dividers between fixtures, since many people will not use these fixtures if it means they will have to be in contact with someone else.

The American tendency to avoid physical contact with strangers provides some important clues about making public seating arrangements more efficient. People consistently avoid public seating that puts them uncomfortably close to others. In selecting seats on a long bench or couch they will occupy the two ends first. Unless they are then joined by friends, the space left in the middle will seldom be used unless someone has a pressing need to sit down. As a result, very long seats are not as efficient as shorter-ones because they will seldom be used to capacity.

Where people are required to sit close to others for appreciable periods of time, as they would on buses or airplanes, or at lunch counters, it is helpful if each seat and each counter section is clearly identified as a separate entity so that there is no question about individual boundaries.

The concept of personal space as a buffer between individuals does not completely cover all aspects of this phenomenon. There is another aspect of personal space that deals with the preference or desire for a place that is identified as one's own. Whether this is a work station, an office, or a bedroom, separate is preferred to shared. An important part of this feeling of possession is the right to personalize. To a large extent, what makes a space personal is the freedom an individual has to adapt it to his or her own needs and desires. This is a point that designers should keep in mind when designing such spaces.

PERSONAL STATUS

Human beings employ a variety of techniques for affirming their own self-definitions and, it is hoped, for defining themselves to others. Their manner of speech, vocabulary, posture, movement, clothing, hairstyles, and tastes are all part of this self-definition, as are the larger and more obvious elements such as the automobiles they drive, the friends they choose, and the homes in which they live.

The use of physical artifacts to affirm an individual's or an institution's status and prestige is at least as old as architecture. Many of the architectural monuments of the past were erected with just that point in mind. It is no surprise, then, to see corporate headquarters buildings rising higher and higher in metropolitan

Personal-space bubble. *People are generally more sensitive to space in front of them than they are to the space behind or beside them.*

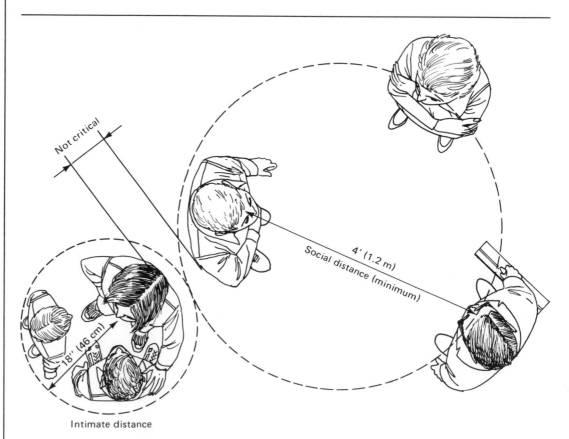

Not critical

Social distance (minimum)

4' (1.2 m)

18" (46 cm)

Intimate distance

Public seating. *People usually select the ends of long seats, leaving the middle sections empty.*

Territorial boundary markers. *Clear boundary markers between positions at the lunch counter and between individual seats in public places reduce one source of annoyance.*

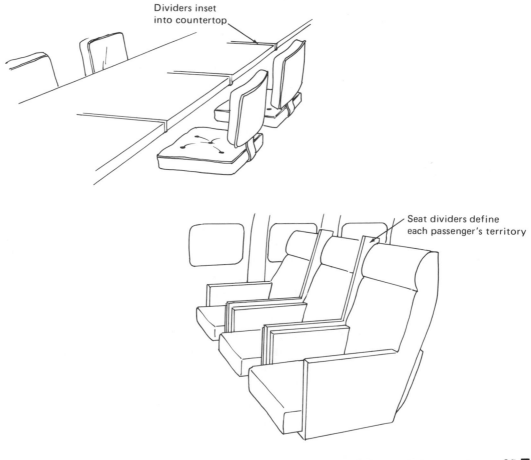

Dividers inset into countertop

Seat dividers define each passenger's territory

centers, or spreading across ever more parklike sites in the suburbs. These are just different manifestations of the same urge.

The owners of such buildings, the clients who commission their design, will seek an architectural expression that will reflect whatever image they consider appropriate. This explains, in part, why there can be such a diversity of architectural expression at one time. Owners may choose to be formal and conservative, low-key and unassuming, casual and relaxed, or outrageously avant-garde. They have only to select an architect who works in that style. If the building design were solely a matter of reflecting the owner's self-image, there would be no limitation on choosing a style. If the building is to communicate some special message to the public, however, as discussed later in the section on *Communications,* the design options may be sharply limited. Avant-garde architectural design that might be readily accepted in a high-fashion clothing store might seem bizarre to the customers in a family restaurant.

While the image or status a building communicates to a viewer is an important part of an architect's design problem, defining the status of the occupants of the building is equally important. It is a widely accepted practice in North America to denote rank or status by the perquisites of an individual's workplace. Private offices, corner windows, carpeting, wall paneling, and furniture quality are some of the means that are used to differentiate people of different rank. Many corporations and public agencies have firm rules on how these amenities are to be distributed.

It is a designer's problem to maintain parity of amenities at each supervisorial or managerial level. While the individuals involved might be personally undemanding about their work spaces, that does not mean that they will happily accept something less than their peers are getting. Furthermore, most workers have a keen sense of what is normal in their fields. Advertising agency employees at every level will have a clear idea of what the employees of other agencies are getting. As a result, it is not only necessary to maintain parity within an organization, it is also necessary to stay close to the norms of the field. Giving them *more* than the norms of the field would not be likely to upset anyone.

In dealing with personal status, the important thing for a designer to remember is that allocating floor space, window locations, furnishings, and other amenities is not just a matter of working out attractive and functional work spaces; it is also the touchy and emotionally sensitive matter of allocating personal status.

TERRITORIALITY

One aspect of human behavior that has been widely reported and discussed is the characteristic called "Territoriality." While comparisons with the defensive behavior of nesting birds or the hunting territory of a pack of animals are sometimes made, the territorial behavior of human beings is complex. It is not limited to the defense of boundaries. It merges with other feelings about personal space and with concern for personal status. Territorial feelings may relate to individual belongings, to group belongings, or to assumed rights and privileges that may be transitory in nature. The principal categories are listed below:

PERSONAL PROPERTY AND POSSESSIONS

Clear examples of human territorial behavior are found in the strong reactions to invasions of personal property boundaries. The home owner who uses his own back yard as a private dump is not likely to tolerate anyone else using it for that purpose. Even if the property in question is only a numbered parking space in an apartment complex, the sense of inviolate territorial privilege is just as strong.

GROUP PROPERTY AND POSSESSIONS

While group territorial feelings may not be as strong as individual ones, they are nevertheless important. They cause us to rise to the defense of "our" neighborhood, "our" team, or "our" town. Since these feelings can help to unify a group of people and thus lead to group action to defend its common resources, they are of special interest to designers.

TEMPORARY TERRITORY

In addition to things that are owned singly or jointly, people sometimes assume temporary rights in places where they have no legal property rights at all. Picnic tables in the park, a place in line at the supermarket, or a comfortable chair at a cocktail party may become "ours" for the moment, and any invasion can create a genuine sense of outrage.

Territorial behavior is evident throughout American society. It manifests itself in many ways, though it is sometimes difficult to identify. To make a complex topic even more confusing, there are times when the *absence* of territorial behavior is a cause for concern. In dealing with the myriad manifestations of this behavior a designer may at one moment be attempting to reduce territorial friction and at the next moment be attempting to encourage feelings of ownership.

PERSON TO PERSON

Most territorial friction arises over personal belongings. This starts at an early age with siblings quarreling over the use of toys. It continues with roommates arguing about whose towel is being used and with co-workers debating the illegal use of a personal coffee cup. These disputes may not be serious, but they can be minimized if personal possessions are clearly marked. While "His" and "Hers" towels won't ensure a serene marriage, they eliminate one possible source of friction.

BOUNDARIES

Disputes over territorial boundaries and the rights within those boundaries erupt with some frequency in suburbia. These can often be traced to ambiguity of the boundary lines. Where the lines are clear and self-evident, problems are minimized. Where facilities are shared, as in the case of common driveways, there must be some means of indicating clearly what is shared and what is private.

Shared facilities can lead to petty conflicts. In apartment living, a shared deck or even shared access to a parking space may be troublesome unless the distinction between common and private rights is clearly made. Merchants who use a common loading dock or share a waste-storage area will have fewer problems if their individual rights and responsibilities are carefully spelled out.

GROUP TERRITORY

The next step up (or down) in the level of territorial sentiments is the feeling of sharing "ownership" of something through membership in a group. Individual ownership rights, in the legal sense, may not be involved. Apartment house tenants, who may have disputes between themselves about their personal rights, will nevertheless join forces to repel invaders who threaten to use the grounds and facilities that the tenants regard as "theirs." The same protective tendency applies to "our" school, "our" neighborhood, "our" office, or "our" street.

The territorial feeling that a group develops about a given locus is especially important to planners, as it makes it possible to mobilize a group to defend or improve its shared territory. Unless the residents of a neighborhood develop strong territorial feelings that will enable them to organize effectively for group action, it is questionable whether the neighborhood can maintain its desirable characteristics over a long period of time. Developing a neighborhood territorial sense is difficult to do, however, unless the neighborhood is recognized as a distinct entity; it must have clear boundaries and must have, or adopt, a distinctive name. It is hard to marshall support for an amorphous entity such as the "west side of town," whereas "Westwood" is likely to attract staunch supporters.

NO ONE'S TERRITORY
A group that feels an identity with a place can help ensure that it is used properly and that it is defended against misuse and vandalism. Places for which no one or no group develops territorial feelings are subject to misuse and abuse. Obvious examples are seen in the vacant buildings, empty lots, and abandoned cars in blighted areas. A more subtle, but more widespread, manifestation results from the assumption of territorial rights by some agency or authority other than the users.

Managers of an institution or an organization may set and post rules for the use of its facilities without involving the actual users in the process of developing them. This is a normal procedure in companies and public agencies of all kinds. The effect is to relieve the users of any sense of territorial responsibility. They may scrupulously follow the rules, but if a drinking fountain overflows and ruins the carpet around it, it is not viewed as their problem because it is not "their" carpet. This situation is commonplace. Designers should be aware that such attitudes can result from any planning venture where decisions are made without involving the actual participants. If there is no involvement or participation, there may be no feeling of responsibility.

Designers might wish that people did not feel so strongly about their territorial rights, real or assumed; life would be simpler in some ways if people were more inclined to share territories. Such thoughts are not very realistic, however, as territoriality is a strong sentiment in most societies and is not likely to disappear in the foreseeable future. By understanding the nature of this feeling, designers can both minimize the friction that results from territorial disputes and maximize its potential benefits.

TERRITORIAL RECOMMENDATIONS
In the following chapters that discuss the places where people live and work, there are specific recommendations made about territorial considerations. There are a few general rules, however, that would apply in most circumstances.

- **Individual possessions.** Mark them in distinctive ways or give them individual names. Whether the possessions are concrete objects or just assigned space in an office, dormitory, or locker room, a designer should clearly define the boundaries.

- **Group territory.** Establish clear boundaries and a clear identity. This is essential for the development of specific group territorial feelings. This is not difficult in small projects but it becomes very difficult, if not impossible, in large projects. The only *certain* way to ensure that group territorial feelings develop in very large projects is to break them down into smaller components with different names and clearly different characteristics. This recommendation is quite at variance with current trends in architecture.

- **Transient territory.** Some transient territorial rights are attached to such prosaic items as bar stools, bus seats, and a place at the urinal in public toilets. We are all better off if such shared facilities can be used without unecessary friction. It is helpful if they can be designed and arranged so that the area assigned to each individual is clearly delimited. This would mean dividers between the urinals, individually formed bus seats, and markers imbedded in countertops.

- **Territorial responsibility.** To ensure that a sense of territorial responsibility develops among users in those projects that actually belong to someone else, as in the case of public institutions or corporate projects, the designer should make every effort to include the users in the planning process. Clearly defined boundaries and a clear identity are not sufficient to ensure that this sense of responsibility will develop. If the users do participate in planning, however, their participation helps to establish the bond with the project.

COMMUNICATIONS

One aspect of humankind's social nature is a strong desire to communicate. People communicate in order to find out what is happening in the world, to exchange information, to determine the attitudes of others, and to express thoughts and feelings. Much communication now takes place through some form of medium, such as the printed word, radio, television, facsimile transmissions, computer terminals, and telephones. In spite of the growing sophistication of electronic communication systems, no technique now available or foreseen can match the precision and accuracy of face-to-face conversation.

In addition to the use of language, humans communicate in a variety of more subtle ways—by means of posture, expression, gesture, and intonation. All these channels are normally used to supplement spoken language, but each one is capable of conveying a message by itself. The fact that all these channels can be brought into play in face-to-face communications is what makes this natural form of communication so effective. It should be obvious, of course, that the use of some medium such as the telephone or a letter cancels out the powerful effect of posture, expression, and gesture, making it much easier to deliver bad news or to deal with highly emotional issues.

Architects and other designers have little to do with the techniques of communication but they have a lot to do with the creation of places where communication occurs. They are involved with communications at three levels:

- **They must provide the appropriate ambient conditions that foster effective personal communications** by ensuring that there is adequate light of the proper type so that facial expressions can be seen clearly and by ensuring that the acoustic environment is such that verbal statements can be heard clearly and understood without distortion.
- **They must provide the appropriate information, principally through signs,** so that people will know how to use the facilities they are entering. This is not easy to do well. Signs must be located in the right place, be easily read, and must communicate some comprehensible and usable information.
- **They must provide, principally through external design characteristics, accurate information** about the nature of a structure and the organization it houses. This is not wholly a matter of signs. A sign may clearly state that the building houses a shoe store. It may or may not indicate how expensive the shoes are or whether it is a good place to buy shoes for children. That information, if it is available at all, is conveyed through other cues such as the openness of the design, the displays, and the nature of the materials. This aspect of architectural design has not been systematically studied.

PERSONAL COMMUNICATIONS

To facilitate communications between people, a designer must recognize that conversations take place wherever people meet. This may be in a formal conference room, or it may be on a street corner. A designer's responsibility for and control over these varied sites is obviously limited. There is, however, a list of considerations that generally apply and should be used as a set of guidelines.

- **In heavy traffic areas,** provide a place where people may stand out of the line of traffic.
- **Provide seating** wherever it appears that chance meetings and conversations may occur with some regularity.
- **Seating should be flexible** so that people can adjust it to suit their own preferences.
- **If seating is not flexible,** it should be arranged so that people can sit at approximately a 90-degree angle relative to each other.
- **Lighting should be arranged to illuminate the faces of people** who are conversing so that facial expressions can be clearly read. This is a consideration that is often overlooked. Much lighting design is focused on objects such as tables, desks, and displays, rather than people.
- **The color of the light should be appropriate,** such that people's flesh tones are rendered correctly.
- **Minimize or exclude outside noises** that might interfere with conversation.
- **Provide an acoustical setting** that is free of reverberation and distortion so that speech can be heard and understood clearly.

COMMUNICATING WITH SIGNS

In using signs to communicate information about a building or a site, a designer must answer some complex questions about what people need to know and when they need to know it. People approach buildings for different reasons. Not everyone needs to know where the loading dock is located. As a consequence, it is necessary to evaluate the needs of the different kinds of people who might approach the building and make certain that their information needs are met.

New buildings, or new building complexes, can be, and should be, organized in a logical fashion that simplifies the sign problem. Older structures or complexes that have been repeatedly altered and expanded pose extremely difficult problems. Major hospitals and college campuses seem to have the tendency to evolve into such complex forms that it is impossible to navigate through them without the

The preferred relationships for communication purposes. *a. Seating that can be moved to suit individual preferences is most satisfactory. b. If seating cannot be moved or adjusted, then it should be possible for the individual to shift or move.*

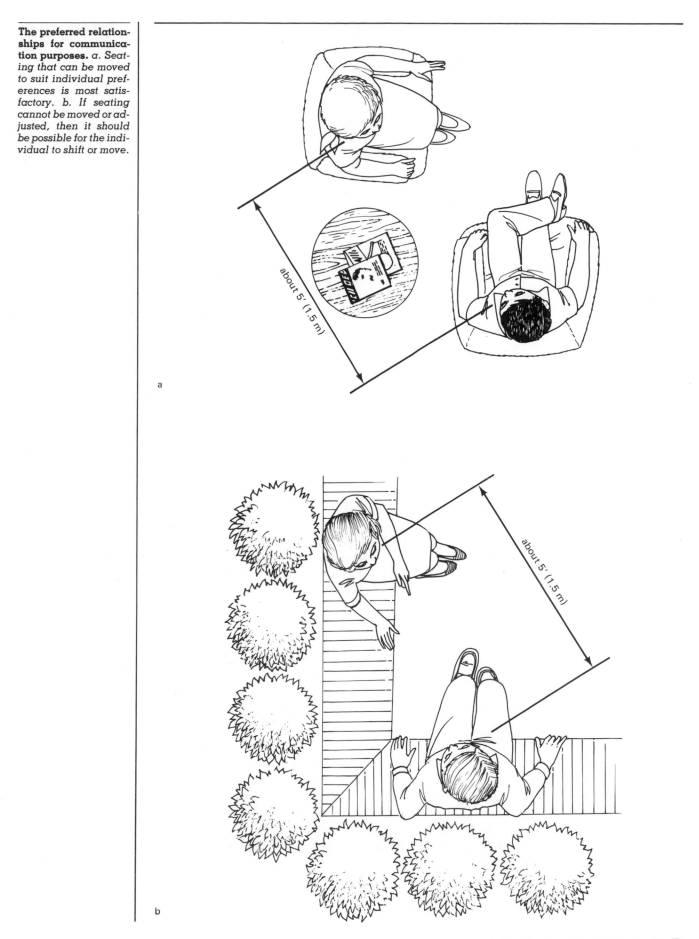

a

b

aid of a pilot. Clear and explicit directional information in such complex surroundings requires patiently tracking each group of potential users through the complex to their individual destinations and the liberal use of "you-are-here" maps, signs, color coding, floor and wall lines, and, where language may be a problem, the use of easily grasped symbols.

COMMUNICATING WITH DESIGN

The last category of communication within the designer's province, the ideas or emotions that are conveyed by the design of a structure itself, is difficult to deal with. Some people find it hard to believe that the design characteristics of a building are capable of communicating any message, but independent studies conducted by Ifan Payne and Robert Hershberger indicate that architectural design does communicate. Unfortunately, both their studies indicate that the feeling or emotion a building design communicates to the general public is frequently quite different from the feeling or emotion that it communicates to a group of designers. In fact, the evaluation of the general public is often exactly opposite to the evaluation made by designers. What is interesting, exciting, or unique to a group of designers may well be bad, ugly, or annoying to the general public. As a consequence, there is little point in discussing communication in such terms.

As a result, the following discussion focuses, instead, on the manner in which people evaluate a building and the organization it houses as a means of satisfying their needs of the moment. In doing so, it is useful to divide people into two groups: those who are familiar with a building and those to whom the building is a new experience. To people who know the building, it becomes part of a familiar background. Their response to its design characteristics is largely a result of how well they feel the building suits their own purposes. Employees will judge the building they work in on the basis of lighting, sound control, heating and ventilation, layout, circulation, and other functional characteristics. Shoppers who are familiar with a shopping mall will judge the mall on the basis of convenience, ease of parking, circulation, price and quality of merchandise, and quality of service. In the eyes of habitual users, architectural character cannot be separated from functional quality. If the building does not work well for them it is not attractive.

For people who are not familiar with a building, the extent to which design elements may communicate useful information is a function of the interests and needs of the individual more than of the nature of the building. Architects and designers in general have a keen interest in the nuances of design, but this is not true of the public at large. For the most part, buildings are background, of interest only if they seem to offer something that would satisfy an individual's needs or interests. If you are hungry and the building houses a restaurant, then the building design can play a part in communicating the nature of the establishment and motivate you either to go in or to look for an alternative. If you are not hungry, whatever message is embodied in the building design is blocked out. The fundamental rule of communication, at any level and in any medium, is that there must be a receiver for the message as well as a sender.

The kind of communication discussed here, where a building design communicates information that is relevant to a viewer's needs or interests, is a complex and elusive matter. It is a critical motivation for newcomers to an area. For people who have just arrived in a new community or a new neighborhood, the external design characteristics of a building are sometimes the only cue that is available to them about the nature of the business or institution housed within. In the course of time, they will learn the favored places to transact business, but their original choice will be influenced by what they can see. This is a critical matter for many kinds of businesses. If businesses can get a customer inside the store, they have a chance to demonstrate the superior nature of their service. If they cannot get the customer inside, the quality of their service is irrelevant.

From the viewpoint of a new viewer, there is a series of questions that a building design should answer so that the viewer may determine whether the building satisfies any current needs or interests.

- What it is?
- What benefit does it offer me?
- How do I get in?
- What is inside?
- How will I be received?

In answer to these questions, a designer has a very limited vocabulary of responses.

- **What is it?** The response is given with either a sign or a symbol. In grappling with this problem it becomes apparent that we have a very skimpy supply of universally understood symbols to work with. The Christian cross and the Jewish Star of David offer an easy and accurate identification for religious structures, but there are very few other symbols with such power. The three gold balls of the Medici family, once used to identify pawn shops, have vanished; so has the red and white-striped pole that once marked barber shops. The gasoline pump is a universally read and understood symbol, but it is hard to extend the list. Perhaps that is why the golden arches of McDonald's and the distinctive logos and trademarks of other franchise operations have played such an important part in their success. The symbol is information; it assures you, for better or worse, of a known quantity.

  If there is no symbol that conveys the necessary information, then the signing must tell the whole story.

- **What benefit does it offer me?** Here again the answer will be conveyed by signs or by evidence. A motel that wants to attract traveling families will display its room rates in neon. A restaurant will display a menu that answers not only the question of variety but also the question of price. Other merchants will display a sample of their wares. The means will vary with the scale. The scale of the signs and symbols that would be appropriate for a pedestrian shopping mall would not be effective in pulling traffic off an interstate highway.

- **How do I get in?** The way into a building and the way into a parking lot must be absolutely clear. If there is a parking lot, the drive to the parking lot should pass the building entrance so that the return path is clear in the mind of the visitor. Signs and arrows are, of course, useful in pointing the way, but this is one instance where symbols may speak louder than words. Parking-lot entrances are easier to find if they are bracketed with pylons, gateposts, or some other substantial, easily seen physical features. Building entrances are also easier to find if they are marked by highly visible features such as canopies, marquees, or other architectural elements.

  Finding the entranceway may not be much of a problem in small structures that can be understood at a glance, but in large complexes such as shopping malls and major hospitals, providing clear entrance information is an important aspect of the building design.

- **What is inside?** The designer obviously has a lot to do with answering this question. Regardless of any arguments that may be advanced in favor of windowless buildings, if people who are approaching the building for the first time cannot see inside, one of their major questions about the building remains unanswered. The use of glass as a means of opening parts of the building to public view does not, in itself, completely solve the problem. If the glass is too dark or reflects the buildings across the street, it may appear as opaque as a solid wall.

■ **How will I be received?** This is a very important question for a viewer and a most difficult question for a designer. It relates to the concern an individual may have about entering a situation that may result in being embarrassed or rebuffed. The question can take many forms. "Does this bank look like one that would welcome large accounts but would be very reluctant to open my small account?" "Does this doctor's office look like one where the staff would be very impatient with me if I asked for help in filling out my insurance forms?" "Does this restaurant seem to be one where we would get a lot of hostile looks if the baby started to cry?"

The openness of an establishment in terms of ease of access and ease of seeing inside helps to answer these questions. Another part of the answers lies in the choice of materials and the scale of the establishment. Obviously expensive materials and furnishings will cause some people to turn away because they may feel ill at ease in such surroundings. That may, in fact, be exactly what the owners and their designers had in mind. Very large banks may also intimidate some prospective depositors and may indeed discourage small accounts.

A designer can only resolve the question of "How will I be received?" by understanding clearly who the building is supposed to serve and establishing a clear and unambiguous identity that will reassure those potential users. The question of how a building communicates useful and reassuring information to a new viewer is one that badly needs further study. It is obviously important to commercial enterprises. Although it may not be so obvious, it is equally important to private and public institutions of all kinds. Yet the design decisions that determine the form of a building are almost always the product of personal preferences rather than a systematic and knowledgeable effort to communicate to the public.

CUE SEARCHING

One very practical need, common to everyone, is the need to know what is going on in the world around us. As a result, people search for cues that will provide the information they need to conduct their personal affairs safely, expeditiously, and with a minimum of wasted effort or embarrassment.

The nature of this search for information takes on different forms at different times. When people enter a new district or a new building for the first time, they do so in an exploratory mode. They proceed cautiously, searching for cues as they go. They are easy to spot at the entrances to many buildings. Most tourists move in an exploratory mode. Once these same people have become accustomed to a new setting, however, they move in an habitual mode. They move briskly, with confidence, and seem to pay little attention to their surroundings. This is a deceptive appearance. While habitués do not need to scan their environment for cues as newcomers do, they are nevertheless very sensitive to changes in their environment, or unusual events or occurrences. An understanding of this behavior is of value to designers. It indicates, first of all, how important information is to the constant stream of newcomers who have no other way to understand and use the streets and buildings they encounter. The second point is that if a designer wants to attract the attention of habitués, it will be done most easily by changing some familiar part of the environment.

One of the principal purposes of cue searching is to ensure personal safety. People count on traffic signals to tell them when to proceed across an intersection. They look to warnings on labels to keep them from ingesting poisons, and they rely on conventional faucet positions to ensure that they will not be scalded if they turn on the righthand faucet in the shower. In these instances people rely on the assumption that someone else has done his or her job properly and that they can safely proceed on the basis of the information they have been supplied. People assume, for instance, that if the green light is their cue to proceed through the intersection, the cross traffic will be looking at a red light. If this is not the case, they may pay a high price for their trust in others.

Many of the most useful cues are natural ones. For instance, the sheen on the sidewalk warns of icy conditions ahead. The rumble of a janitor's cart coming around the corner causes us to hug the side of the corridor to avoid a collision. A change in texture underfoot from carpet to concrete signals that we are on the public sidewalk and had better take the necessary precautions. All of these cue-reading sensations reflect survival skills that are part of our evolutionary equipment. They were critical for the survival of our ancient forebears and they are no less critical for human survival in the streets of a city. The great difference today is that people are exposed to a number of hazards they are not equipped to sense. New materials, new equipment, and new systems are encountered whose nature is unknown and thus cannot be inferred from experience.

A designer can do a great deal to make cue searching more effective and more accurate. The first step is to provide facilities where the senses can work, where there is enough light to see, and where the ambient noise level is low enough so that critical sound cues can be heard. The next step is to avoid sensory overload. Some buildings, such as busy airport terminals, offer so many new sensations and so much new information that these cues cannot be processed effectively. In such cases perceptions may be overwhelmed and people will miss the important cues they need. The cure for sensory overload is to stress the critical information and to subordinate everything else.

The last step for the designer to take in order to facilitate cue searching is to provide direct guidance in the form of signs and symbols that warn the public of hazards and guide them to their destinations. At this point, *Cue Searching* begins to merge with *Communications* in a special category called *Wayfinding*.

WAYFINDING

One of the skills our forebears had to develop was an ability to navigate across a landscape devoid of roads, road signs, maps, or helpful service-station attendants. It was and is a remarkable skill, but it is of little value in trying to navigate around an apartment complex, across a college campus, or through the maze of corridors in a large hospital. No doubt each of these examples is perfectly logical to the architect or planner who developed the plan and probably poses no problem to the people who have become accustomed to it. Someone who is trying to navigate in a complex building for the first time, however, may find it completely incomprehensible. Such people clearly need wayfinding assistance.

The first rule of wayfinding is that nothing is as helpful as a knowledgeable human being who has been assigned to assist strangers. An information center or a trained receptionist is more effective, and will be consulted by more people, than any combination of direction signs and maps.

In circumstances where it is not possible to station a receptionist, a "you-are-here" map should be displayed. Properly located and oriented, such maps can be very helpful. They should be horizontal if possible, correctly oriented for the viewer, and relate to some obvious landmark in the immediate vicinity.

"You-are-here" maps should be supplemented with other wayfinding systems. In large building complexes there should be clear sign identification on each structure at eye level where it is well lighted, has good background contrast, and is

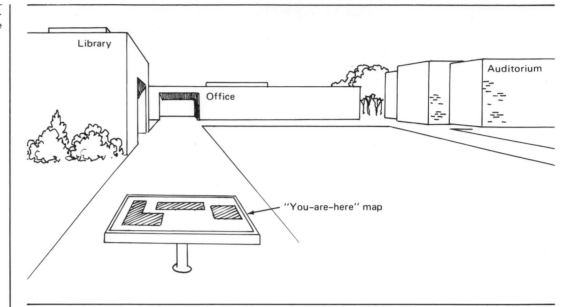

"You-are-here" map

large enough to be seen and read from any normal line of approach. This may require more than one sign. Color coding may be used to identify certain wings or departments in a building. Color coding plus signs can be used to identify each elevator lobby in a multistory building so that when the elevator doors open it is immediately obvious what floor the elevator is on. Lines may be laid out on the floor or on the walls, directing traffic to specific destinations. It must be made clear, however, what these lines mean and where they lead. In addition there should be periodic reinforcement in the form of signs to indicate that the traveler is still moving in the right direction.

Signs remain the most versatile and widely used aids to wayfinding. They must be well lighted, at eye level, large enough to read from normal approach distance, in a legible typeface, and on a contrasting background. The most important consideration of all is that signs should convey a useful, understandable message. So far as wayfinding is concerned, the content is much more important than the form.

ABSTRACT CUES

In addition to the visual and auditory cues that help us understand our environment and navigate through it safely and efficiently, there are cues that inform us about social status and create the mental images we hold of both people and institutions. This class of cues has been an important factor in architecture throughout recorded history. The rich and powerful of all ages have sought to project an image of their wealth and authority by the grandeur and opulence of their buildings, sometimes called the "edifice complex."

The edifice complex is alive and well today, and its effect is visible in every city in the land. Large organizations and institutions build vast headquarters structures to house their operations and demonstrate the scale of their resources. Smaller organizations lease part of a big building and then rent the sign space at the top of the building to create the impression that it is all theirs. The edifice complex has been a boon to the architectural profession.

The conventional cues that suggest status on the exterior of a building are scale, quality of material, aloofness, and maintenance. Aloofness refers to the sense of separation from other structures and distance from the public way. Interior cues are material quality, low noise level, ceiling height, door height, and the quality of

The importance of sign legibility. *It is impossible to read the departmental sign, which is on the glass to the right of the doors, because it is seen against the confusing background of an abstract painting.*

The importance of sign content. *The departmental sign can now be read against the blank wall, but seeing it doesn't help much. The message "Books and Reading" is of little value in finding something in a large university library.*

the decorative elements such as carpeting, wood paneling, lighting fixtures, and hardware. The concept of "quality" as used here refers to an individual's perception of that characteristic. The general public does not hold the same views about material quality as the design professions.

The status cues discussed here are to a large extent determined by culture and are subject to modification as a result of changing fashions.

PERSONAL SAFETY

One characteristic that is universally considered to be a fundamental cornerstone of human nature is a concern for personal safety. This does not mean that people will not take risks. It means, rather, that people will not *knowingly* take risks unless there is some reward involved, either in the form of some material gain or some psychological reward. To attempt to cross a busy street without looking for oncoming traffic would be to take a great risk without any compensating benefit. Normal people do not take such risks.

There are many hazards, however, that people are not well equipped to evaluate. New kinds of materials and chemical compounds, new kinds of equipment, or new applications of old materials may pose hazards that the average individual cannot evaluate on the basis of past experience. Human beings do not possess the sensory mechanisms that would make it possible to recognize dangerous radiation, or to identify toxic chemical components that may be released by familiar household products if they are ignited. Nor would experience prepare them for the hazard of stepping off a moving sidewalk without being prepared to absorb the shock of transition from a moving surface to a static one.

People obviously need help in identifying those aspects of their environment that may be hazardous even though the hazard is not obvious. People also need help in identifying those aspects of their environment that may be safe even though they may not appear to be safe. So far as the built environment is concerned, designers have a primary responsibility to resolve both of these concerns. The designer, in other words, is responsible not only for creating a safe environment but also for making it apparent to the user that it is safe. The importance of such psychological reassurance in encouraging people to enter and use new environments should not be underestimated. Not everyone is young, mobile, and self-confident. Many older people, pregnant women, people with physical disabilities, and even young people who are ill or injured may be reluctant to enter strange, new areas where they may be uncertain about their ability to move safely.

The range of potential hazards that might be encountered in the buildings, parks, and streets of the city is far too great to be dealt with here. The list that follows is confined to some of the principal categories of hazard that are encountered frequently:

- **Clearance hazards.** This refers to the fact that buildings are hard objects, much harder than people. Any space where normal people will not fit, such as under open stairs, should be made inaccessible.
- **Object hazards.** There are many objects in the streets and buildings of a city that are potentially hazardous because their edges and corners are sharp. Cabinet edges, desk and counter corners, corridor corners, traffic sign posts, and a host of other everyday objects would be much safer to live with if their edges were rounded and softened.
- **Collision hazards.** People collisions may be as injurious as car collisions. There is nothing that can be done about people who do not look where they are going, but the designer can at least make it possible for those who do look to be able to see. This injunction applies to both pedestrians and drivers. Wherever traffic

streams meet, at parking lot entrances or in office corridors, there should be a clear field of vision so that oncoming or crossing traffic can be avoided.

- **Stability hazards.** One frequent cause of injury in homes, in buildings, and on streets, is slippery surfaces underfoot. These may be in the bathtub or shower at home, on the sidewalk outside, or on floors and stairways in any building. Potentially slippery surfaces should be avoided. Where circumstances require that a slippery surface be used, as in providing a sanitary surface for baths and showers, grab bars should be installed at convenient levels for use by people of all ages. Handrails should be used on any ramp or set of steps, no matter how short.

These are by no means all the hazards of modern life, but they represent categories of hazards that are not usually covered by building codes and are easy to overlook.

In addition to the elimination of the actual hazards listed above, a designer has an added responsibility to reassure building users that they have nothing to fear. Frequent sources of such fears are heights and steep steps or ramps that appear to create a danger of slipping or falling. These fears can affect people who are concerned with their own safety as well as those who are concerned for the safety of others. Parents might feel personally safe with the handrail around an open deck but have great fears for the safety of their small children.

Extensive areas of plate glass, extending to the floor with no safety rail, are viewed as very hazardous by many people. If the glass is of an appropriate type, this condition may not, in fact, be hazardous; however, if people perceive a thing to be so, it is so as far as their feelings and actions are concerned. There are many reports of people in high-rise buildings with floor-to-ceiling glass who will not approach the glass, but confine their movements to the area along the inner walls. No designer would knowingly create such a stressful environment, but it is very easy to do so unknowingly.

4 | LIVING TOGETHER

Humans are social beings. In the first months of life they cannot survive for more than a few days alone. As adults, their normal mode of life is in company with other human beings. They live together in small family groups, clans, tribes, villages, towns, or cities. Rarely do they live in isolation. Indeed, condemning an individual to solitary confinement is one of the harshest penalties our society can mete out.

While group living is normal for human beings, it is also a source of stress. Friction between individuals results from sharing the same rooms, the same buildings, the same streets, and the same towns with people who have different values, interests, and habits. It seems ironic that, while we might avoid some of our problems if we chose to live apart, we stay together in the social tradition of human beings. The benefits of group living are compelling.

Many sources of personal stress are beyond the influence of even the most gifted designer. Indeed, there are relatively few that are subject to design influence at all. Even so, an understanding of the stress sources that *are* subject to design influence can lead to worthwhile improvements in family and community life.

When we think of group living, we usually think first of homes and apartments. While these are certainly the primary settings for group living, they are not the only ones. Wherever people live together for extended periods common problems are likely to appear. The locations may be as diverse as military barracks, college dormitories, summer camps, or isolated outposts such as oil-drilling platforms. This list of settings for group living can be expanded in an important way by adding the neighborhoods where we live.

The use of the words "living together" should be defined for our purposes as meaning living close to others; it does not necessarily mean sharing the same quarters. It is especially important to make that distinction at this time because of an emerging trend that may substantially alter the nature of American housing in the years to come. A growing percentage of young people, having left school, are living in separate households. At the other end of the scale, a growing number of single elderly people are occupying separate households. A predictable result is that a substantial portion of new housing will be designed for single occupants.

Certain human goals and values should be paramount considerations in designing the places where people live together, wherever those places may be.

PERSONAL SAFETY

A sense of being secure is an integral part of the concept of a home. Specifically, it means security from the elements as well as security from intruders. For families with small children, it also means assuring the safety and well-being of their offspring. Concern for personal safety extends beyond the home or apartment. It includes the safe use of outdoor spaces and safe passage to and from the home.

TERRITORIALITY

Certain territorial problems attach to home ownership or to apartment living. Clear boundaries outside the house help to minimize friction between neighbors. Clear territorial boundaries within the house are equally important. This is especially true, for example, when siblings share a bedroom, although it is also important when any family members must share work or social space within the house.

PERSONAL SPACE

The fact that individuals choose to live together rather than in isolation does not eliminate their need for privacy. All forms of housing should provide someplace where an individual can achieve personal privacy. It is strange, and unfortunate, that in many homes and apartments the only place where privacy can be ensured is the bathroom.

PERSONAL STATUS

A regard for personal status is intimately bound up with an individual's choice of housing. The exterior appearance of a house and its grounds, and the manner in which they are maintained, have a great deal to do with the initial choice and with the feelings of satisfaction experienced from living in it.

FRIENDSHIP FORMATION

Though friendships are based on shared interests and backgrounds, they are formed within the group of people we know and are in contact with. Our contact group is, largely, a result of where we live and where we work. It is also affected, however, by the way in which our apartments, houses, workplaces, and neighborhoods are arranged. Making it possible for people to make contact or to avoid contact as they choose should be an important consideration for designers. Unless there is a chance to meet, neither friendship nor acquaintanceship is possible.

AT HOME

Nuclear families consisting of a mother, father, and offspring continue to be the basic units of American society. While it is a social unit with a history as long as humankind's, it is not free of stress. Parents are concerned about their relationships with their offspring, but they also have a need to nurture their own relationship. With more than one child in the house, sibling conflicts are a problem. These stresses and the universal concerns of personal safety, territoriality, and personal status make it apparent that the design of a family dwelling involves much more than simple utility. Each of the concerns discussed below are essential planning criteria.

PERSONAL SAFETY

The starting point for the design of a house must be a concern for the security of the inhabitants and their possessions. At some time in the past it may have been possible to take security for granted, but that is not the case now. Actually, the designer has two security-related concerns: first, that the house be functionally safe for the occupants, and second, that the occupants *perceive* themselves as being safe.

There are several aspects of personal security. Each requires a different planning solution.

- **Security against forcible entry.** There are a number of devices and systems to protect a home against forcible entry. From a behavioral standpoint, the best protection is the interest and concern of the neighbors. The following recommendations stress that approach to the problem.

1. Houses that are clearly visible to the neighbors and that permit them to observe suspicious activities benefit from this surveillance.
2. Neighborhoods where the houses are oriented to the street and where there are usable front porches and considerable street activity also offer more protection.
3. Mutual protection will only be effective in communities where there are people at home during the daytime.

- **Children's safety.** Monitoring the safety of small children and carrying out other household duties simultaneously is a common parental problem.
  1. Provide a playspace for small children in the area where the parents spend a large part of their time, such as the kitchen. A playpen may be used, but there must be some place to put it that does not interfere with other parental activities.
  2. Provide an outside play area that is protected from intruders and animals and that can be supervised easily from within the house. Lack of such an arrangement causes considerable stress for parents.

- **Household safety.** The home should be a secure haven for families or individuals. Instead, private dwellings are the scenes of an alarming number of disabling accidents. Without attempting to enumerate all of the safety concerns that a designer should be aware of, it should be remembered that homeowners are not all young and agile. Endurance and agility decrease with age, pregnant women lose some of their coordination and mobility, and young and old alike are sometimes ill or incapacitated. As a consequence, some rather prosaic precautions are stressed here because they are overlooked so frequently.
  1. Eliminate slippery floors, showers, tubs, and stairways.
  2. Large areas of plate glass, particularly on upper floors, are frightening to some people even though they may be quite safe. Install obvious grab bars and handrails.
  3. Provide barriers at all clear glass openings that extend to the floor so that people will not attempt to walk through them.
  4. Sharp edges and sharp corners on cabinets, counters, furniture, and equipment of all kinds should be eliminated.
  5. Electric devices, heating equipment, and cookstoves must be installed so that children cannot reach them, and must be maintained in a safe condition.
  6. Backout driveways should be avoided or kept short, with unobstructed rear vision, to avoid injury to people and pets.
  7. Some means of escape must be provided from each bedroom in case of fire. Household fires are a significant hazard in multistory housing, particularly on hillside sites.

TERRITORIALITY

Territorial feelings may be most evident at home. Territorial problems are the basis for neighborhood feuds and sibling disputes. While many neighbors live in relative harmony, certain circumstances can cause friction even between old friends. Defining territorial boundaries is reasonable insurance against future disputes.

- **Define boundaries.** To avoid misunderstandings, make it clear where one property ends and another begins. Territorial feelings are not limited to land tenure, however. They extend to belongings as well, particularly such potentially annoying possessions as pets. As a consequence, if personal pets may be a problem, fence them in (or out).

Mutual surveillance. *Neighborhood security is improved if houses are designed properly and are close enough together.*

Safety for small children. *The household work center should have an overview of the children's play area.*

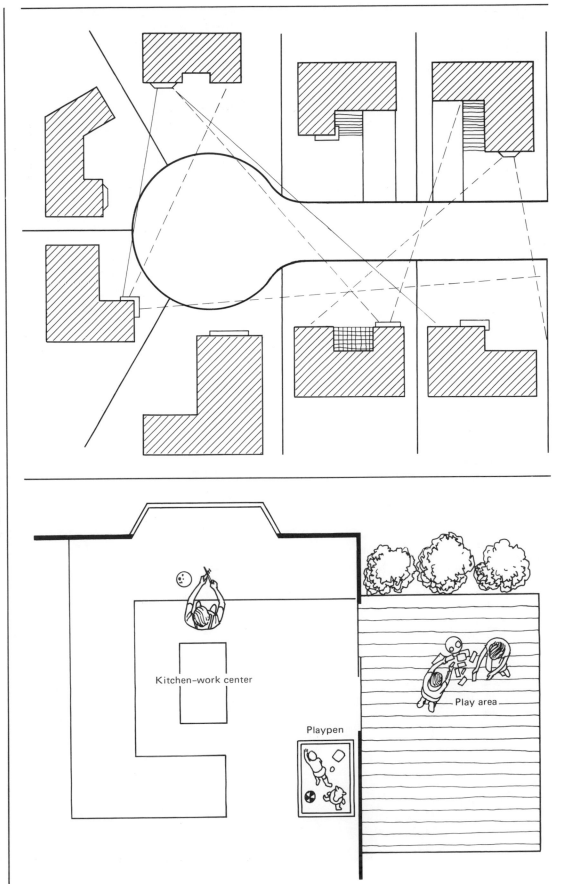

Kitchen–work center

Playpen

Play area

Identify territorial conditions. *The designer should distinguish between private, shared, and public spaces and facilities.*

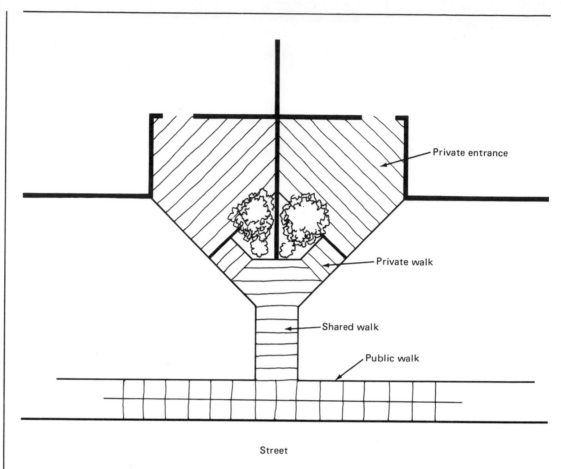

Private entrance

Private walk

Shared walk

Public walk

Street

Shared rooms. *Space and facilities should be clearly defined and divided between the occupants.*

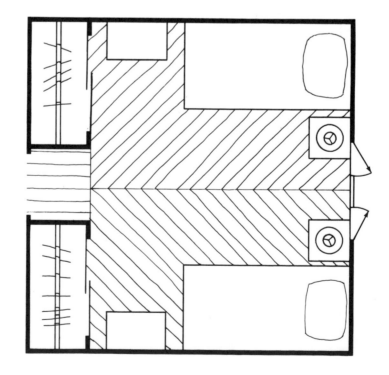

- **Define shared spaces.** Where walks or driveways are shared, what is shared and what is private must be clear. Shared spaces should be designed to facilitate cooperative use by the neighbors. The street is clearly shared, and when street parking is permanently appropriated for a private motorhome or boat trailer, strong disagreements can result. Sharing problems become more sensitive as housing is moved closer together. It is particularly important in condominium projects, where private property outside the doorway may be measured in inches rather than feet.
- **Define shared rooms.** Where rooms are shared there should be a clear division of spaces and facilities between the different occupants. While such divisions will not eliminate sibling strife, they at least provide a basis for adjudicating disputes. Countless children have survived shared rooms, closets, chests, toys, and beds, but a clearcut split of available resources reduces friction in the children's room.

PERSONAL SPACE

Family life and community life both require an ability to get along with others. Getting along with members of the family is in some ways training for getting along with members of the community. There are times, however, when anyone may feel a need to be alone. While housing standards in North America are spacious compared to those in some parts of the world, it is nevertheless hard to find privacy in many American homes. As a result, the bathroom and the automobile, two most unlikely places, have become private retreats.

- **The parents' sector.** In addition to the need for individual privacy, there is a need for parents to have a place for shared privacy where they can discuss their intimate concerns, pursue shared activities, and where they can love freely. There is no special formula for the design of a parents' room that could be counted on to nurture intimacy but the following characteristics are very important.

  1. The parents' room should be remote from the children's area.
  2. It should be acoustically isolated to provide privacy for personal discussions, disagreements, lovemaking, and other intimate behavior.
  3. It should be comfortable from the standpoint of temperature, ventilation, and furnishings.
  4. It should be possible to control both daylight and artificial light.
  5. It should be adjacent to a bath for both ritual and hygienic purposes.
  6. It should have the nature of a special retreat for the parents. They may share it with the children as they choose, but it remains their special space with clear, unmistakable boundaries.

  In addition to their need for shared privacy, parents, especially working parents, need someplace at home where they can work without interruption. Without a private place to work at home, working parents tend to spend more time at their workplaces and less time at home. As a result, it is important to provide a private adult work area—either a separate study or a separate part of the bedroom.

- **Privacy for the rest of the family.** Ideally, each family member should have some private space for a retreat. If this is not possible, there are some compromises that can be helpful.

  1. The territories in shared bedrooms should be clearly divided.
  2. Locks should be provided on all bedroom doors. Where small children are concerned, privacy locks that can be opened easily from the outside should be used.

House zoning. *Clearly zoned houses and apartments make it possible for parents, as well as their offspring, to find some degree of privacy.*

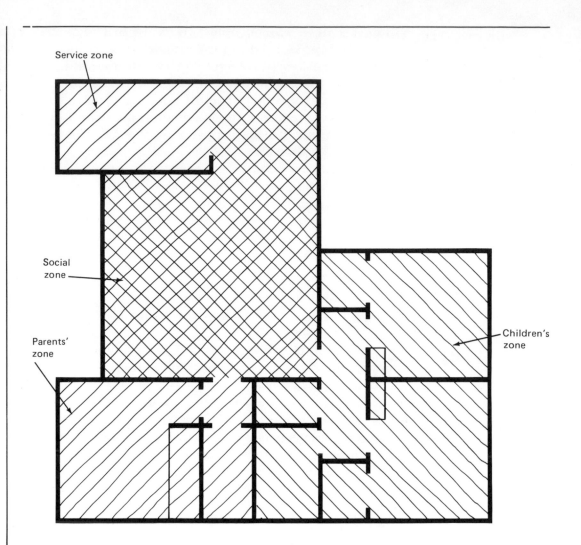

Service zone

Social zone

Parents' zone

Children's zone

Divided bath. *A divided bath increases the opportunity for privacy.*

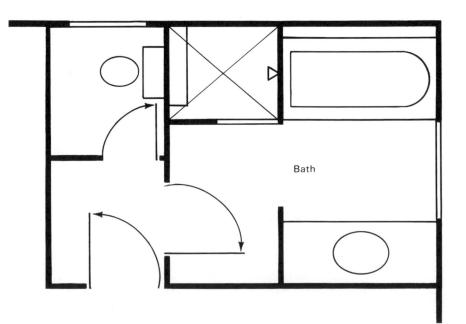

Bath

3. Divide the bathroom into two sections. The bathroom is a busy place in households with children, partly because it serves disparate needs. Bathing is an admirable activity in our society, cleanliness having connotations of luxury and sensuousness as well as godliness. Elimination, on the other hand, is something our society prefers to keep out of sight. The fact that these two disparate activities share a common space in most homes is due to the chance circumstance that both require plumbing connections. An extension of this logic would put the kitchen sink in the same room. A more rational approach would put the toilet in a toilet room and the bath in a bathroom. The house would then have two spaces where an individual might expect some degree of privacy.

4. Provide more small-size rooms rather than fewer larger rooms. A common characteristic of current housing is to compensate for smaller overall size by combining rooms into a few larger spaces. The result is a more spacious appearance and housing that is better suited to adult living and entertaining than it is to family living. A family generally will be better served with more separate spaces, permitting a wider range of activities to take place with greater privacy.

PERSONAL STATUS

Somewhere very close to the sense of territoriality is the sense that our possessions and our surroundings reflect our personal statuses or contribute to the images of ourselves that we hope others will accept. It is sometimes assumed that all Americans aspire to an image of material prosperity and elevated social status, but this is not always the case.

Some people seek to fit the norms of a neighborhood, whereas others want to stand out. Some avoid ostentation while others make certain that the world is aware of their standing. In view of this disparity, there are few universal guidelines for designers to follow.

A designer working with an individual client will, of course, react to that client's special concerns. A designer creating housing for rent or sale to an unknown client has a more difficult problem. One helpful fact is that, in selecting a home, an individual's sense of personal status is reflected in a concern for the neighborhood's standards of maintenance and upkeep.

- **Make marketing studies.** There is no way to predict accurately how prospective buyers in any given market will evaluate the appearance of a house without marketing studies to test the response to the design.

- **Incorporate low maintenance materials and design features.** If each homeowner can maintain the house at neighborhood standards without undue effort or expense, the chances of attracting purchasers who approve of those standards is increased.

- **Provide each house with screened areas for outdoor activities** that might affect the status of the neighborhood. Sometimes people like to do things outside that are distasteful to their neighbors. Neighborhoods vary in such standards. Nude sun-bathing would be unacceptable in many areas; overhauling automobiles on the front lawn, building boats in the side yard, or parking motor homes in the street would also be unacceptable in many areas.

FRIENDSHIP FORMATION

Securing membership in a definite social group is important to most people. Securing membership in that special social group we know as the neighborhood is especially important since it has a great deal to do with reciprocal commitments to personal security and joint efforts for the benefit of the neighborhood as a whole.

This last point will be discussed in detail later in this chapter, in the section dealing with the neighborhood. Before any joint action can take place, however, people must be on speaking terms. There are several steps that can be taken to encourage this result.

- **Reduce sources of friction.** People who are constantly at odds with each other are not likely to become friends. A designer needs to ensure that territorial boundaries are clear, as previously described. Make it possible for each home-owner to take care of the prosaic utilities of everyday life without annoying or offending the neighbors. Provide a suitable place for the rubbish to be put out for collection, a place to hang heavy garments (or strip cars) outdoors where the neighbors cannot see them, and a place where household pets can eliminate without invading someone else's turf.

- **Increase the options for pleasurable and beneficial contact.** Even the friendliest of people would be happy not to have to greet their neighbors with a broad smile on every occasion. Flying out the front door in pajamas to put out the trash before pickup time and walking out stealthily in the same garb to get the morning paper are two occasions when anyone might prefer to avoid an idle chat. There are many more times, however, when a conversation with a neighbor can be a helpful and encouraging interlude. It is worthwhile for the designer to pay careful attention to providing opportunities for contact.

- **The approach and entrance to the house should be visible from neighboring houses.**

- **Provide an area in front of the house where it is convenient and comfortable to sit outside.** If people are sitting in front on a porch or sheltered terrace, the chance of making contact as the neighbors come home is improved.

- **Provide an area in front of the house where small children can play with parental supervision.** Small children at play attract other small children — and their parents.

- **Preserve privacy options with a protected back or side yard and a protected access to the garage and car.** Once in the car, it is not normally required that you stop and talk unless you are specifically flagged down by a neighbor.

In considering how a design solution may influence friendship formation, it should be remembered that while physical closeness is an important factor, functional closeness — the likelihood of being brought into contact at the bus stop, at the mail box, or while mowing the lawn — is much more important.

IN AN APARTMENT

Apartment living, and to some extent condominium living, are special subsets of living in single-family homes. Much of what has been discussed in the preceding coverage of *AT HOME* will apply here and should be reviewed.

While apartment living and condominium living differ somewhat because of different territorial attitudes associated with owning versus renting, they are similar in regard to density and to their relative openness to public access. These factors are important matters for the designer who is concerned with the behavioral aspects of design. They will be discussed as they relate to the group of attributes discussed at the beginning of this chapter.

PERSONAL SAFETY

All the personal-safety concerns discussed earlier apply equally to apartment living. To some extent they are intensified because of the characteristics of most apartment buildings. Apartment buildings are frequently more than one story high, so that the hazard to life and property from fire is greater than in most

Outdoor-space alloca-
tions. *Provide a front
social area and a pro-
tected private outdoor
space. A screened area
should be provided for
projects and activities
that might seem un-
sightly to neighbors.*

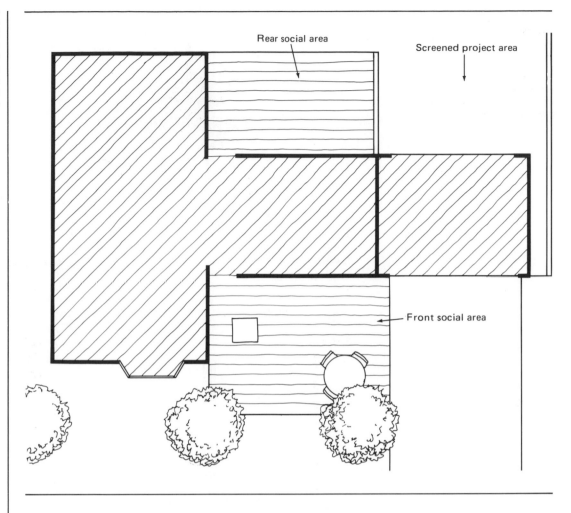

Rear social area

Screened project area

Front social area

single-family residences. Because apartments are occupied by clusters of people living in close quarters, a substantial amount of traffic is generated by visiting friends, relatives, tradespeople, and deliveries. As a result it is hard to distinguish between legitimate traffic and intruders.

In some urban areas apartment-house crime is a serious problem — one which is difficult to solve without introducing all the paraphernalia of gates, locks, and security guards. Without a formal security apparatus, apartment-house dwellers must rely heavily on mutual surveillance for protection. This is reason enough for neighbors to know and get along with each other. Here are some considerations that will help promote apartment security.

■ **Build low-rise buildings.** Apartments of three to four stories in height seem to be inherently safer than high-rise structures. Low-rise buildings that permit parents to see play areas next to the building also relieve parental anxiety about the safety of their children.

■ **Provide security systems.** If high-rise structures are absolutely required, they should be provided with tight security control at *every entrance*. This includes garage and basement entrances, service entrances, stair-tower exits, as well as the more formal entrances.

■ **Cluster apartments around a common entrance or stairwell.** This arrangement offers several benefits. It increases the opportunity for contact with other residents so that there is more sense of personal involvement and mutual concern. It also makes it easier to recognize who "belongs" in the entry.

Clustered apartment entrances. *Tenants can be more conscious of entrance activities if there are windows into the entry area and clear territorial identification of each apartment entrance.*

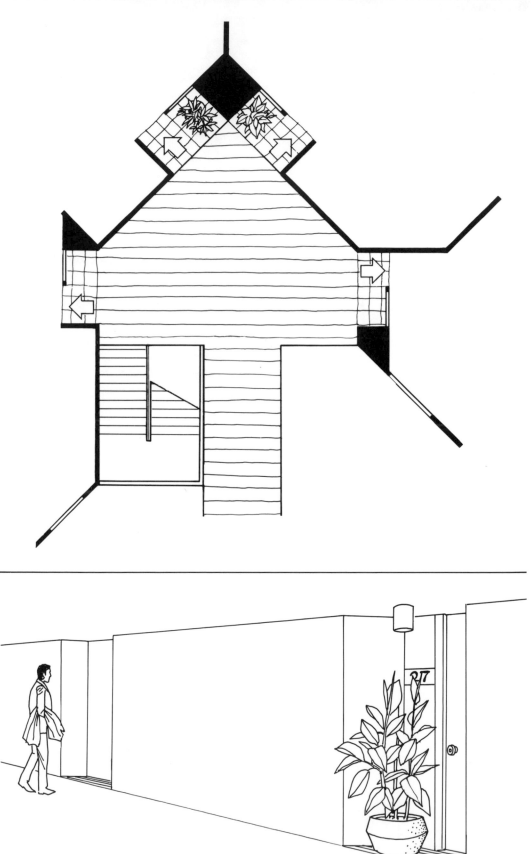

Apartment unit entrances. *Each unit should have a distinctive entrance instead of just a door.*

- **Avoid long, double-loaded corridors.** In their usual form they are a "no-man's land" that doesn't belong to anyone and for which no one assumes a territorial concern.
- **Create an "entrance" at each unit.** Each individual apartment or condominium should have a distinctive entrance. The entrance should be designed so that people in the apartment can have the option of seeing out into the corridor, stairwell, or elevator lobby. The entrance design should also provide that part of the space in the corridor or passageway be assigned as part of the individual apartment's territory. The purpose of this proposal is to encourage the residents to assume some proprietary concern for at least part of the public space and what goes on there.
- **Tenants should have a view out through their entry into the corridor that serves them.** They should also have windows that permit them to see the approaches to the building and the ground area.
- **Clearly define the project territory.** The grounds and approaches to the building should be clearly defined so that it is obvious when a person moves from "public" territory to "project" territory. This can be accomplished with grade changes and landscape development as well as by gates and physical barriers.

Boundary markers. *The boundaries between "public" territory and "project" territory should be clearly defined.*

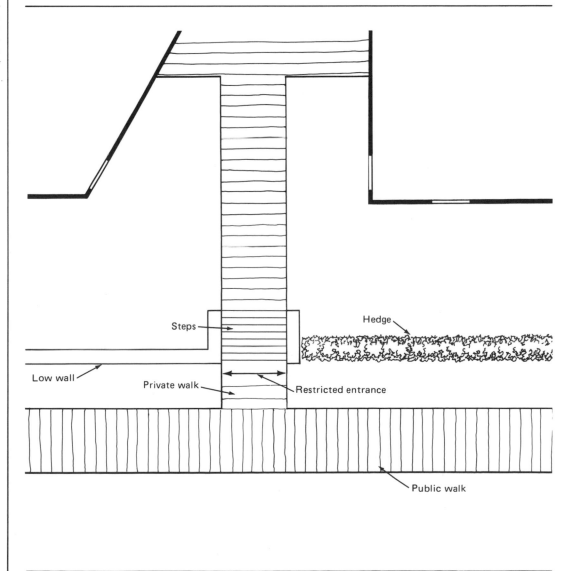

Steps

Hedge

Low wall

Private walk

Restricted entrance

Public walk

TERRITORIALITY

As far as the interior of the apartment unit is concerned, the territorial considerations should be exactly the same as those previously discussed under the *AT HOME* heading. As far as the balance of the building and the grounds is concerned, there is no difference in principle but there is a great difference in details.

In any leased or rented structure there exists an obvious dichotomy between the territorial feelings of the owner and the territorial feelings of the tenant. The interior of the apartment unit is clearly the tenants' "territory," but only in a limited way. These limitations must be spelled out in the lease or rental agreement. Rental agreements, which are usually drawn up by the landlord, should reflect an understanding of the territorial feelings of the renter and recognize that, for the most part, the landlord gains in security and upkeep of the property if the tenants develop a strong territorial attachment to their quarters.

Tenants themselves divide an apartment-house environment into two categories — "mine" and "ours." In addition to the interior of their own apartment unit, they may claim as their own any parking stalls or garage space designated for their exclusive use, private storage units, and any exterior space adjacent to their unit that was clearly intended for them. The balance of the building that is accessible to and generally used by the tenants falls into the shared or "ours" category. It is important to both owners and tenants that the "ours" feeling be strongly developed. This sense of participatory ownership encourages the tenants to be concerned with the overall well-being of the structure. Certain measures encourage this feeling.

- **Define boundaries.** Make certain that those elements that are the private territory of the tenant are clearly marked. Parking stalls and storage units should be numbered or named. Apartments should also be numbered and provision made for the tenants to display their names at their entrances if they choose to do so. Any outside space assigned to a tenant, such as a terrace, porch, balcony, or the entry area in the corridor previously described, should be distinguished from others by color, pattern, texture, or other special treatment.
- **Define shared spaces.** Places that are shared by all tenants should be identified by color, texture, furnishings, or some other distinguishing characteristic so that they are obviously separate from places that are the personal preserve of individual tenants.
- **Define areas inside the apartment.** The same rules apply here that apply inside the home. Where rooms are shared, there should be a clear distinction between the spaces and facilities that are for common use and those that are the property or territory of each occupant.
- **Define the boundaries of the development.** An important part of the security program described earlier requires that both the public and the tenants be absolutely certain about the dividing line between the public right-of-way and the area that is part of the apartment project. This is a critical requirement for controlling access.

  If it is considered appropriate to invite the public into the project, then the same kinds of territorial markers that were previously discussed should be used to direct the public to the appropriate areas and to make it clear where they are welcome and where they are not.

PERSONAL SPACE

Where privacy between the members of the family is concerned, the requirements in an apartment house are no different from those in a single-family dwelling. As far as privacy between dwelling units is concerned, the problem in the apartment is more severe and more difficult to deal with. Acoustic and visual privacy are the primary concerns. Visual privacy for tenants, when they are outside their own apartments, is only rarely available. Tenant surveys indicate that lack of privacy, especially acoustic privacy, is regarded as one of the most annoying drawbacks of apartment living.

If privacy is hard to find in the average single-family home, it is an even rarer commodity in the average apartment. The desirable goals in an apartment parallel those discussed in greater detail in the preceding *AT HOME* section.

- **The parents' sector.** It should be remote from the rest of the family and be visually and acoustically private. It should be close to a bathroom for both ritual and hygienic purposes.
- **Working privacy for parents.** Working husbands and wives require some place at home where they can work privately. If this is not available, they will spend less time at home. A separate study, shop, or studio is ideal, but if that is not possible a separate workplace in the bedroom is a useful substitute.
- **Privacy for the rest of the family.** Under ideal circumstances, everyone in a family should be able to retreat to some private space. The designer of a custom home can address that problem directly. An apartment house designer cannot be so specific because the actual inhabitants of a given apartment cannot be known in advance; furthermore, they will change in time. There are some strategies that will definitely help.
  1. Arrange and equip each bedroom to permit clearly assigned territories for at least two occupants.
  2. Provide privacy locks on all bedroom doors.
  3. Separate bathing facilities from toilet facilities. Providing more than one bathroom will also help, but it is not an efficient substitute for having separate access to a bath and a toilet.
  4. More small-size rooms are better for family use than fewer larger rooms.

PERSONAL STATUS

Just as the homeowner seeks to establish a measure of personal status in selecting a home, the apartment dweller seeks the same thing in renting an apartment. The appearance of the apartment community is, in fact, a leading concern to prospective renters. The district, the neighborhood, and the street are all part of this concern, but the actual appearance of the building and grounds and the care with which they are maintained seem to be the primary interest. If these aspects of the project discourage prospective renters, they may never see the interior features, no matter how desirable they may be. It appears that the public tends to rate desirable exterior appearance in terms of upkeep rather than specific architectural style.

While appearance is clearly an important matter to apartment renters, it is hard to extract specific guidelines for the designer. The building or buildings should clearly have an attractive and distinctive appearance, but such adjectives mean different things to different people. A distinctive name for the project would be helpful, but what might be regarded as attractive in one neighborhood might be laughable in another. There are few recommendations that can be made with certainty.

- **Conduct marketing studies.** This is the only way to determine if a design will appeal to potential renters in a given area.
- **The building should be built of materials that will be perceived as durable and permanent** *by the public*. This is an important distinction, since the public

perception of such qualities is not necessarily the same as that of building professionals.

- **The building materials and the design should convey the impression that the apartment interiors are quiet and private.**
- **The building and grounds should be designed so that they require only a modest amount of maintenance to retain a quality appearance.**

The exterior characteristics discussed above have very little to do with long-term satisfaction with an apartment. They are important factors in a renter's initial evaluation of a building, but unless the units themselves accommodate a family's needs comfortably and effectively, renters are not likely to be satisfied for long.

FRIENDSHIP FORMATION

Living in a large apartment structure, even with its dense concentration of people, can be a lonely way of life. If a resident's travel is limited to taking the elevator down to the garage in the morning and back again in the evening, the chance of making social contacts along the way is remote. Unless there is some pattern of movement that brings people into contact, density in itself has no effect on friendship formation.

An important factor in social exposure is functional distance. Families in adjacent apartments may live only inches apart, separated by just the thickness of the common wall, but if they use separate entrances or move on a different schedule they may never see each other. They are functionally close only when their paths cross and their activities bring them together.

There are people in many apartment houses who have no interest in making friends with their neighbors and who are primarily interested in protecting their privacy. The designer will, of course, have to make that option available to them.

On the whole, tenants have a great deal to gain from forming a network of acquaintances even if they do not become close friends. Sharing is in many instances both effective and rewarding. Car pools, baby-sitting pools, and shopping pools can make life a little easier. On a cold morning when the car won't start, it is a comfort to know someone who is willing to help. Even more important is the fact that a network of friends and acquaintances is a tenant's best assurance of security. In a properly planned facility, friends and acquaintances provide the mutual surveillance previously discussed under the heading of *Personal Safety*.

Some of the recommendations made earlier under the heading of *Personal Safety* are equally important in providing opportunities for friendship formation. Indeed, the reason they contribute to personal security is that they generate social contacts and lead to the creation of a mutually supportive social fabric in an apartment complex. The suggestions that follow all tend to create situations that bring people into contact with one another.

- **Design small buildings or break large projects into smaller segments.**
- **Cluster units around separate stairwells or entries.**
- **Focus traffic in an apartment structure into a common entry.**
- **Make the entry an information center for the project.** Provide a bulletin board for announcements and notices that tenants might want to post.
- **Locate service facilities that are used in common, such as laundry rooms, adjacent to the entrance and just off the main stream of traffic.** Design the space to be attractive and comfortable as well as convenient. The intent is to put these facilities in a prominent location so that they will be comfortable and appealing as well as safe to use.
- **Provide a secure area for small children to play** where their parents can watch them. Children are a common link between families.
- **Provide a common lounge or recreation room.** Include amenities that would

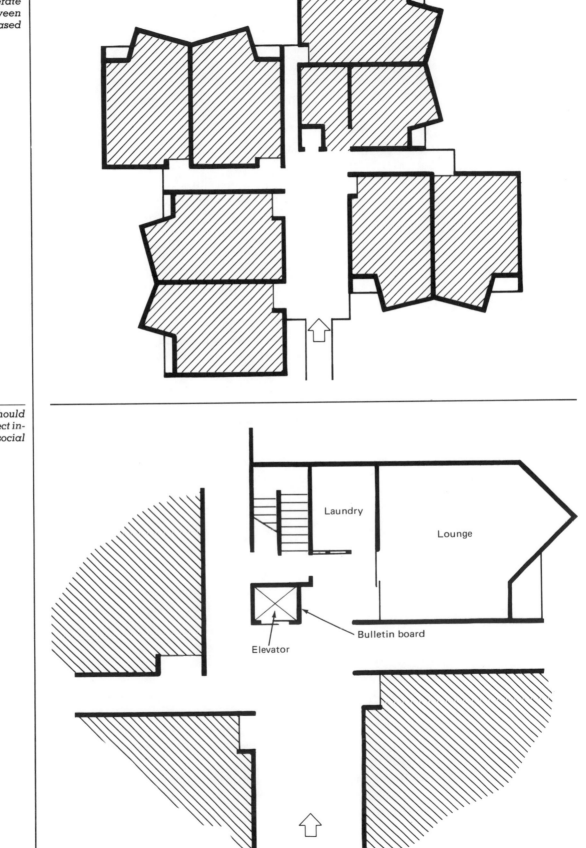

Clustered apartments. *Low-rise apartment clusters without long corridors can generate more contact between tenants and increased security.*

The entry area *should function as a project information and social center.*

Laundry

Lounge

Bulletin board

Elevator

not normally be found in the individual apartment units, such as a fireplace or large-screen TV. This should also be adjacent to the main entrance.

■ **Provide a distinctive entrance,** with an individual nameplate, to each apartment unit instead of the standard anonymous door in an anonymous hallway.

Apartments are built in a great range of types and sizes. In this condensed discussion of the behavioral factors that a designer should be concerned with there has been no effort to make that distinction. The principles apply universally, but the details that are appropriate for larger projects would require some modification for smaller projects.

IN A DORMITORY

While dormitory housing does not affect a very large percentage of the population at any one time, it is a persistent housing type and one with some special characteristics. While it is usual to think of dormitories in connection with education institutions, especially colleges and universities, very similar facilities are used for military barracks, work camps, and offshore drilling platforms.

At least in the beginning, dormitory living pairs up relative strangers in close quarters, a situation that can create difficulties. At the same time, dormitory life is capable of initiating lifelong friendships. Successfully mixing individuals with different habits and schedules requires a design that makes clearcut assignments of territories and pays close attention to the details of layout and equipment that will permit one person to sleep while another works or studies.

In planning a dormitory, special thought must also be given to the problems of socialization. Individuals who enter a dormitory for the first time are usually entering an entirely new social scene at the same time. Their best hope of affiliating with a recognizable social group is within the dormitory community. The arrangement of the facilities will have a great deal to do with the newcomer's chances of making contact with others and thus learning the local "culture." As was previously discussed, functional distance plays an important part in socialization. If common facilities are arranged properly, people will be drawn into contact with a variety of potential friends and acquaintances. If not, their social contacts will be limited.

PERSONAL SAFETY

It may seem redundant to return once more to the topic of Personal Safety, but contemporary society is plagued by a distressing amount of violence and property crime. Dormitories do not escape these problems. To some extent, because of the easy informality that characterizes dormitories, they are more vulnerable than other types of housing. Again defensive design calls for the kind of facilities listed below that encourage the formation of a sense of community and interdependence. The value of locks and guards is not questioned, but these alone may not do the job.

■ **Build low-rise buildings.** Not only have low-rise buildings been found to be inherently safer than high-rise buildings, but low-rise buildings can be configured in ways that are difficult or impossible to duplicate in taller structures. This is not to say that high-rise structures cannot be made secure, but the cost and the attendant loss of freedom of movement would be especially inappropriate in dormitories.

■ **Cluster units around a common entrance or stairwell.** This is a classic form for college dorms. If the room entrances are designed so that they afford a clear view of the traffic in and out of the dormitory, building security will be improved.

- **Limit building access to the principal entrance.** While fire safety and exiting requirements may make it impossible to adopt this recommendation literally, an effort should be made to come as close as possible. The design principle involved is that entrance traffic be limited to the minimum number of points so that those points can be observed more closely.
- **Avoid loop corridors or long corridors of any kind.** Loop corridors make it possible to enter one way and exit another. While this is an attractive option in many ways, it is not good from a security standpoint. Long corridors, assuming that they serve many units, reduce the degree of involvement of the people resident on them.

TERRITORIALITY

As in the case of apartments, there is a disparity between the territorial rights of the organization or institution that owns the dormitory and the territorial rights of the tenants. The dormitory tenant's rights are transient, of course, but nonetheless important. They must be carefully spelled out in the regulations that govern the use of the building. In developing these regulations, it is important for the owner to keep in mind that it is desirable from every point of view for the tenants to have a territorial feeling about their temporary home.

Since most dormitory accommodations do not provide private toilets, showers, laundry facilties, or kitchens, the tenant's personal domain is limited to the dorm room itself — which is usually shared with one or more roommates. As a result, the category considered to be "mine" is very small but the "ours" category is rather large. This may explain why the experience of dormitory living is so diverse, ranging from loneliness and isolation to a rewarding experience that is remembered fondly. It also illustrates how closely related human characteristics are.

Our individual security is influenced by the territorial feelings developed by our neighbors and roommates toward the common shared space. The fact that we share such territorial feelings results from friendship formation and being assimilated into a recognized group. These important human concerns are all linked, and are all influenced by the design of the dormitory. It is encouraging to know that a building design can contribute to such a beneficial relationship.

- **Clearly define the territorial boundaries within shared dormitory rooms.** Provide distinctly separate facilities for each occupant — separate closets, desks, lamps, bookcases, and beds. Provide an equal share of amenities such as light, ventilation, and view. The design should indicate clearly which areas of the room are the preserve of each individual. While the designer may stop short of drawing lines on the floor or using floor coverings of different color or texture, the distinctions should be obvious to each occupant.

    These recommendations may seem to put undue stress on territorial considerations. Many people do share rooms with little friction, though they may have to submerge occasional feelings of annoyance or frustration. It is this kind of accommodation that makes group living tolerable. The purpose of clear boundaries is to keep annoyance and frustration to a minimum. Thoughtful and considerate roommates can make all kinds of special accommodations. They may ignore territorial boundaries if they choose. The designer's concern is to provide a clear territorial framework in case it is needed.

- **Clearly define the common territory assigned to the each living group.** Any group of people that is to act in concert as a group must be able to identify itself as a defined set of individuals with common attributes and interests. It is easier to identify with a small number of people than with a large number. The maximum number who can achieve a "we" feeling varies with both people and situations; but for a dormitory, 50 residents sharing a common unit is an appropriate size. The number might be increased if the unit were composed of smaller subunits. This would require that large dormitory projects be broken down into smaller segments. Each segment should have the following characteristics:

1. A separate entrance
2. A separate stairway
3. A separate lounge or social center
4. A separate laundry or utility area
5. One or more toilet rooms and shower rooms
6. A distinctive design identity

PERSONAL SPACE

Privacy is as important to dorm residents as it is to anyone else, but it is usually much harder to obtain. Dormitory or barracks living implies being surrounded by people. Being alone, or sharing private time with someone else, is normally not considered to be an option. If privacy is needed, it must be sought somewhere else.

In this regard, dormitories fail to provide for an important human need. Oddly, there is no particular design reason that this should be true. It would be a simple matter to provide the kinds of privacy rooms described below.

■ **Provide private spaces that can be reserved by individuals.** Whether they are considered to be for study, letter writing, meditation, prayer, or simply getting away from the world, such spaces would serve an important need. They can be very small rooms providing a place to sit, a place to write, and the requisite utilities such as light, heat, ventilation, and electrical outlets.

■ **Provide private spaces that can be reserved for couples or families.** There are many kinds of exchanges within family groups or between individuals that are severely hampered by an audience. They range from proposals of marriage to arguments about family finances. If a dormitory purports to provide a surrogate home, it should make some provision for private parlors or courting rooms. They need not be luxurious. They should accommodate four people comfortably with appropriate seating, a small table, lights, heat, and ventilation.

Privacy rooms and parlors.

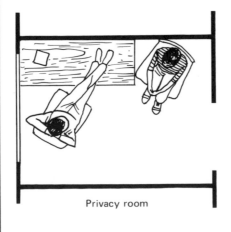

Privacy room

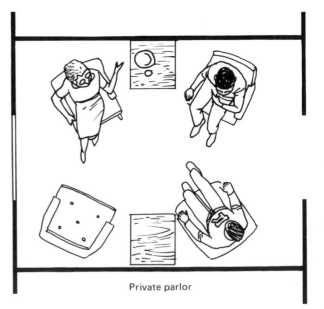

Private parlor

FRIENDSHIP FORMATION
GROUP MEMBERSHIP

Living together in dormitories often leads to the formation of long-lasting friendships. Considering the random process by which entering students are assigned roommates, this seems a surprising result. In actuality, the process is not quite as random as it appears. At the university and college level, at any rate, a certain degree of selection has automatically taken place simply because the student population is not a random sample of the general population. If a group of people are brought together who share common backgrounds and interests, group living is a fertile ground for forming friendships.

Given a suitably designed structure, the impact of the first year in a college dorm on friendship formation is profound. In a study of dormitories at Princeton, F. Duncan Case found that sophomores chose their roommates from among the group who shared common facilities in the freshman dorm. Furthermore, this effect persisted through the senior year. The operative factor was having shared common facilities as freshmen.

Facilities that encourage the formation of friendships are similar to those that were previously described to enhance personal safety. The linkage between the two should be made clear. Friendships do not result from design features that enhance personal safety. The reverse is true: Design features that tend to increase personal contacts lead to safer premises. The type of facility that encourages the formation of friendships is safer because friends look out for each other.

The inclination to seek membership in an identified group is a natural extension of the search for friendship. Being assigned to an identifiable dormitory unit is a step in this direction, but this in itself it does not accomplish the intended purpose. "Membership" is an elusive status; just being a member of the crew doesn't make everyone a shipmate. A designer should seek to create a dormitory that provides opportunities for people to meet and talk with one another, that is small enough that the residents can know each other's interests and concerns, and yet is large enough that there are social options. The recommendations listed below cannot insure that everyone will interact happily, but they will make interaction more likely.

- **Organize the dormitory unit around a group of approximately 50 residents.** If larger structures are required for other reasons, they should be broken into units no larger than this size.
- **Provide an entrance that focuses traffic in and out of the structure.** The entrance should be both a traffic center and an information center. It should contain private, enclosed phone booths and a bulletin board for announcements and the exchange of personal messages.
- **Provide a lounge–social center and a utility area immediately adjacent to the entrance.** This arrangement places important common facilities at a point where traffic is concentrated to increase the opportunity for contact.
- **Place toilet rooms and shower rooms at locations where they concentrate traffic in the sections they serve.** These rooms, usually thought of only for their utilitarian functions, are traffic generators and should be deployed to increase contacts.
- **Provide an entrance at each dorm room rather than just a door.** The entrance should provide a place for each occupant's name if they choose to display it and should make it possible for the occupants to see out into the corridor from inside their rooms.

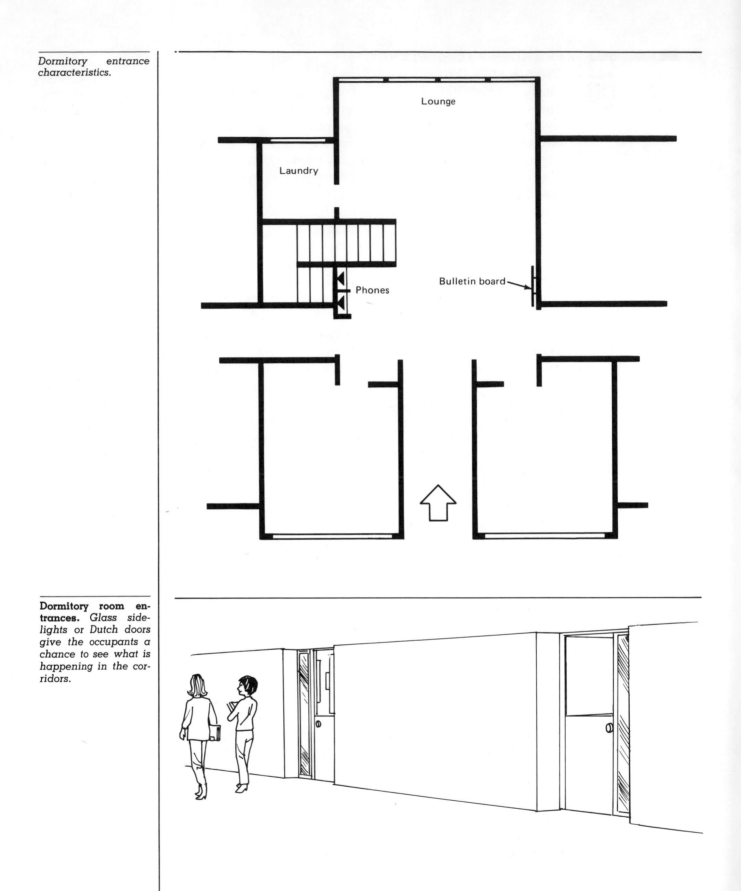

Lounge

Laundry

Phones

Bulletin board

Dormitory room entrances. *Glass sidelights or Dutch doors give the occupants a chance to see what is happening in the corridors.*

IN THE NEIGHBORHOOD

The term "neighborhood" is one that is used loosely both in common parlance and in the planning field. It is freely used in connection with dense, inner-city districts and such astronomical concepts as "the planets in the neighborhood of the sun." For our purposes we are more interested in the fact that people who live in a district may have a concept of their neighborhood that is quite different from that of people who do not live there. Outsiders may associate a neighborhood with some physical feature, a specific set of boundaries, or a historic name. Residents may have no knowledge at all of these factors and think of their neighborhood in terms of the area near home that is well travelled and familiar. If these residents live on a long street with no cross streets, and leave the area for church, schools, and shopping, their neighborhood may be just the one street. If the street pattern provides easy cross-connections, and the essential community services are distributed at various points within easy reach, the neighborhood may be quite extensive.

Most new neighborhoods in this country are created as a result of the activities of development firms who subdivide land into residential or apartment-building sites. The purpose of their enterprise is to create the kind of neighborhoods that appeal to prospective purchasers. The characteristics that make an area appealing to prospective buyers or renters are important, but they are not the only ones that need to be considered. Areas that are desirable from an adult point of view are not necessarily equally desirable places for children. Both of these concerns are dealt with in the recommendations listed below. They are closely related to recommendations made earlier under the headings of *AT HOME* and *IN AN APARTMENT*.

PERSONAL STATUS

The nature and appearance of a person's home, whether a private dwelling or an apartment, is one of the elements that defines a person's status both in that person's eyes and in the eyes of others. The location of the home is just as important in this regard as the home itself. Location is a critical factor in determining real-estate prices. It is the basis for the ageless axiom that the three fundamental factors in determining real estate value are: 1. Location. 2. Location. 3. Location.

Determining the precise design characteristics that make a location sought after in this sense is not entirely a matter for rational analysis. An emotional factor is involved in which sentiment and symbolism, as well as history, play a great part. Even to many who have never seen them, names like "Back Bay," "Greenwich Village," and "Malibu" suggest not just neighborhoods but interesting life-styles. There is no set of rules that can create such images overnight. There are, however, some characteristics that are universally attractive.

■ **The designer can consider the following characteristics as useful guidelines for designing attractive neighborhoods:**

1. Definite boundaries that are well known to the residents and are identified by a name that is known in the community.

2. Houses that do not appear to be too close together or too crowded. Actual distances are influenced by the considerations discussed in the earlier *AT HOME* section.

3. Construction materials and methods that are perceived by the public as being durable.

4. Good maintenance. Maintenance and upkeep are very important indicators of neighborhood quality in the eyes of the public.

5. A pleasant ambience. Attractive neighborhoods will not be noisy; they will not carry heavy traffic on the local streets; and they will be free of disagreeable odors and fumes.

There are other functional characteristics that make a neighborhood attractive, such as public transportation, good schools, convenient shopping, playgrounds, and so on, but most of these are not normally within the purview of the designer.

FRIENDSHIP FORMATION

The *AT HOME* section discussed at length the design characteristics of individual homes that encourage friendship formation. The recommendations for creating a neighborhood plan that encourages friendship formation are surprisingly akin to those suggested for apartments or dormitories. It is important to recognize, however, that neighborhood characteristics that might encourage adults to get acquainted are not necessarily of value to children in their efforts to make friends.

- **Develop a street pattern with short blocks to improve access.** Cross-streets open access to people on adjacent streets instead of limiting contact to the people on the same street. This is especially useful for children, although it is also beneficial to adults for car pooling and other forms of sharing.

- **Provide local neighborhood shopping.** Local grocery stores, drugstores, and hardware stores provide opportunities for social contact. If the street system is properly laid out and is safe for pedestrians, local shopping provides increased mobility for both adults and children.

- **Provide small-scale play areas within the neighborhood.** Parks and playgrounds are generally considered neighborhood assets unless they beome so big, or attract so many outsiders, that they are no longer uniquely related to the neighborhood. If playgrounds provide for large-scale athletic activities, team sports, and organized leagues, they may be so dominated by teenagers and larger children that small children may be excluded. Small-scale play areas are especially intended for small children. The importance of these areas to children is demonstrated by their ingenuity in appropriating otherwise unused spaces for their play activities. A small patch of grass where parents can play with their children is desirable, but even a wide place in the sidewalk would be useful.

A small-scale play area. *Any leftover space can be useful to small children.*

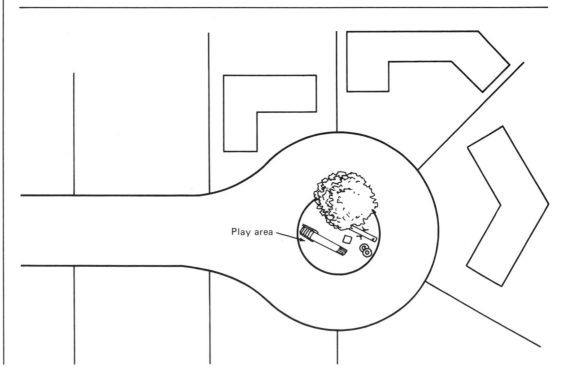

Play area

PERSONAL SAFETY

The amount of land an individual uses for housing purposes is often associated with social and economic status. Small houses on small lots are associated with lower status than big houses on big lots. Even higher on the status scale are houses that are widely separated from each other, set well back from the street, and located in secluded settings (the category we call estates). Housing of this sort provides an unusual degree of privacy for its owners; to many people, it represents the upper levels of status and prestige. A neighborhood characterized by the latter kind of housing is especially hard on children. It makes no pretense at all of being neighborly and, as a result, it is especially vulnerable to burglary. An estate can be fortified to deal with the threat of burglary but the attendant cost, equipment, and personnel are both annoying and burdensome.

One reason that human beings historically clustered together was for their common defense. At present, we may need to return to the same defensive posture. The nature of the neighborhood has a great deal to do with how safe any of us will be. At a time when many women were at home a large part of the day, it did not require many neighbors to serve as a neighborhood watch. Because more houses were occupied, they could be a little farther apart. That situation, however, has changed. With fewer people home during the day, there must be more houses within view of each other to insure that someone will be watching neighborhood activities. That is why the following recommendations are concerned with visibility and sight lines.

- **The success of any neighborhood in reducing criminal depredations will depend on mutual surveillance.** Neighbors must feel enough concern for their mutual welfare that they are interested in what is going on; they must be able to see if a crime is being committed and feel enough involvement to initiate action to deal with it.

- **A house must be visible on all sides from other houses in the neighborhood to discourage forcible entry.** Each house and the approach to each house should be clearly visible from the houses on each side, the house in the rear, and at least two houses across the street. Landscaping should be open so that it does not obscure either the building or its approaches.

WORKING TOGETHER

If "home" is the only arena for human activities that comes close to being universal, "workplace" is, at least, its closest competitor. In western societies it is customary to think of the two as a duality: Work is what we do to support home and family; home is where we rest to ready ourselves for work. While the nature of the work we do is undergoing a change, the stress we experience in working does not seem to diminish.

Solitary workers can arrange their workplaces to suit themselves and do not have to adjust to the needs of others. Most of us lack that freedom. Working generally means working with other people who may differ from us in many ways and are not always compatible. Coupled with the fact that work implies some degree of accomplishment, of tasks undertaken and completed, the workplace can be very stressful.

Certain tasks that have been rigidly structured define work stations that offer very little flexibility in adapting to an individual's preferences. The checker-cashier in a supermarket works at a station that is highly efficient and completely interchangeable. Any checker may operate any station. The person adapts to the station. There are many more instances, however, where operating requirements are not nearly so precise, where individuals might alter or modify their working arrangements to suit their personal needs without reducing their effectiveness or productivity.

Personalization of workspaces may even increase productivity, but in many circumstances that is an option that workers do not have. For some reason there is a widely held assumption that overall efficiency in the workplace demands uniformity and rigid organization. Desks, consoles, and work tables are to be marshaled in ranks and files. The free spirit in the insurance claims department who elects to face a desk in the opposite direction from the herd will almost assuredly encounter stiff high-level resistance. Yet this need to personalize, to individualize, is a frequently expressed desire of American workers.

Adapting the workplace to the worker in order to reduce stress and frustration on the job is the concern of this chapter. Ideally, we should discuss workplaces of all types, but the research data that are available focus on office environments. This is probably a result of the rapid emergence of white-collar office work as the principal source of employment in this country. While employment in this field has increased rapidly, productivity per person appears to have declined rather than increased—in spite of some impressive breakthroughs in office automation and information processing. It is possible that improvements in productivity will not come from further automation but from workplaces that are more satisfying from a human standpoint. Such an effort should be well worthwhile.

Ronald Goodrich, who has studied the problems of the office environment from the standpoint of the users, has calculated that over the life span of the typical office building about 90% of the costs incurred are for employee salaries and benefits with the other 10% being for the design, construction, and operation of the structure itself. Money invested in the building to make employees more effective can have a very high payoff.

While workers are concerned with, and influenced by, all the behavior characteristics discussed in Chapter 3, some of these factors are especially important in the workplace.

PERSONAL SPACE

While few workers experience real privacy on the job, most have expressed a strong desire for some control over their personal workspaces. This feeling is frequently thwarted by the way most workplaces are designed and equipped.

PERSONAL STATUS

The perquisites and amenities that are provided for a workplace are frequently the most visible evidence of an individual's standing within an organization. If these are distributed unfairly, it may create a strong sense of injustice within a working group.

TERRITORIALITY

Workers may have no legal territorial rights at all in their workplaces, but that does not mean that they have no territorial feelings about them. Clear boundaries are just as important in the workplace as anywhere else.

FRIENDSHIP FORMATION

Many friendships form at the office or at the shop. In small groups where everyone has some contact with everyone else, friendships will form if they will. There is no need to utilize any special strategy to bring them about. In large organizations this is not true. The designer owes it to the workers and the organization to arrange facilities that encourage friendly contacts. Contacts made in the lunchroom or on rest break generate a network that constitutes the informal structure of the organization.

GROUP MEMBERSHIP

This is an extension of the need for individual friendship. Most people seek to associate with a group, and the informal networks established by such groups can be beneficial to an organization. Size, however, can be a problem. In small organizations contacts tend to be informal and personal. In large groups they are likely to be bureaucratic and impersonal. This undoubtedly explains the widespread preference among workers for smaller working groups. Designers should strive to create smaller work groups in order to encourage group affiliation.

THE PERSONAL WORKPLACE

"Going to work" is a regular ritual for most adults in this country. Whether they view this prospect with pleasure or dread, when they arrive they will spend their working hours in a physical setting that is provided for them by their employer and over which they have little if any control. If it happens to be well suited to their needs, they are in luck; if it is not, they will have to adapt as well as they can.

Certain assignments are so closely tied to specific equipment or activities that the arrangement of the work station is necessarily restricted by those needs. Working at the ticketing and baggage check-in counters at an airport are in that category, as are most bank teller positions. Most secretarial and clerical work is not so restricted. It presents no real problem if the people involved in this kind of work have more freedom in arranging things to suit themselves. In either situation, the recommendations that follow should be implemented as far as possible.

PERSONAL SPACE

One of the most frequently expressed desires regarding workplaces is the right of individuals to exercise more control over both their immediate surroundings and personal access. While true privacy is not usually available to most workers, there is no reason why limited forms of privacy should not be generally available. Obvious exceptions are those job assignments where an individual serves as an information source or is involved directly with the public. There are several things that could be done to give employees some measure of control over their personal environment.

- **Identify each individual's workplace.** Provide a name plate slot or stand to identify the occupant of each work station. This is especially important in stations where the occupants rotate, as in a checkout stand. Name identification is important to the occupant and to the public that may deal with the occupant.
- **Provide lockable personal storage.** Every employee should have a lockable storage space for small parcels, lunches, or personal belongings. This is especially necessary in any station that is shared on a rotating basis.
- **Face oncoming traffic.** Arrange work stations so that normal traffic approaches from the front, i.e., the 180 degree sector the worker is facing. Above all, avoid placement that permits traffic to approach from the rear.
- **Avoid traffic concentrations.** Do not locate work stations at points where traffic is concentrated, unless the station is to serve as a reception or information center.
- **Provide local control over light and heat.** Assuming that the general lighting level is adequate, most workers would prefer task-specific lighting that they could control to suit their own preferences for direction and intensity. The same applies to heat and ventilation. Both of these proposals are at odds with current tendencies in office design. Providing task-specific lighting is not difficult, but providing local, individual, control over air conditioning may be hard to accomplish. In case this is impossible, the designer should at least ensure that air conditioning is controlled from within the workers' general area. Avoid like the plague automated systems that are controlled by a remote computer.
- **Provide window views.** Locate each work station so that the occupant can see a daylight view through outside windows. This is a strongly expressed preference among workers in a variety of work conditions.
- **Provide flexible furnishings.** So far as the workers assignment permits, work-station equipment should offer each individual as much flexibility as possible. Work-station requirements vary too much to permit specific recommendations, but generally there should be one principal work surface, one secondary work surface, a connecting area for equipment, and special storage such as shelves, drawers, or bins for whatever material is dealt with. All of these units should be adjustable as to height, and relation with each other. "Standardizing-to-the-mean," on the assumption that one size can be used to take care of everyone, doesn't work any better with office furnishings than it does with socks.
- **Provide for personalization.** Unless there are serious policy problems that prevent it, every work station should provide the means for personalization. This means that each individual should have an opportunity to keep close at hand the trophies, photos, miniature plants, postcards, or other mementos that he or she feels comfortable with. This recommendation may seem to upset the dignity and decorum of business and professional offices, but if it is taken as an essential part of the design criteria it is not difficult to accommodate.
- **Provide for ease of cleaning.** Any work station should be designed so that it can be easily cleaned and easily kept in that condition. This is especially impor-

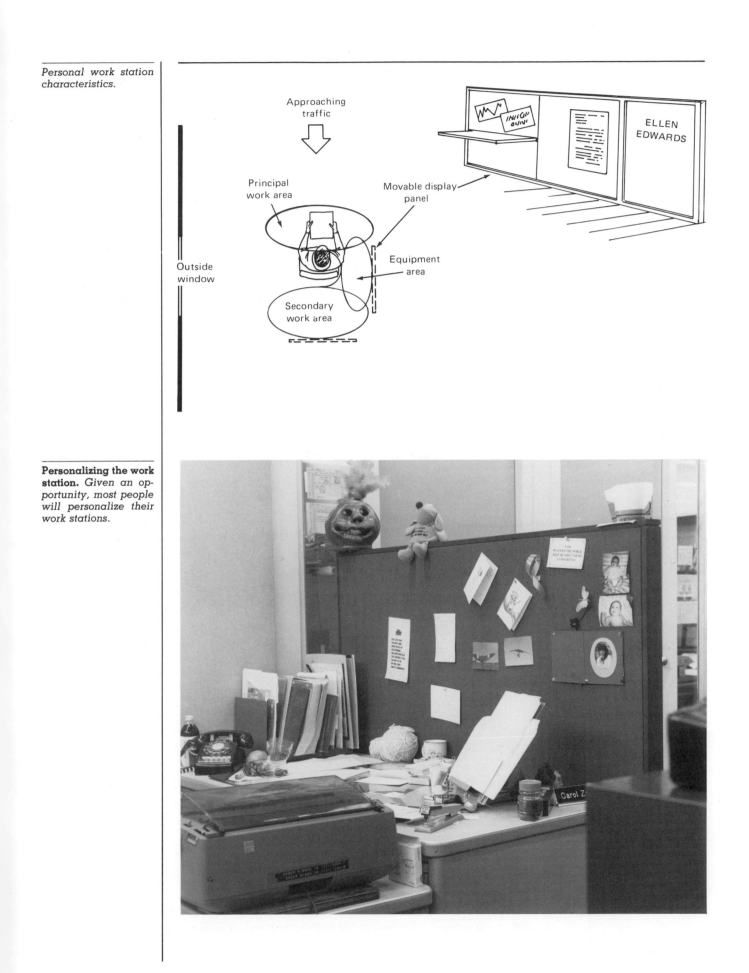

Personal work station characteristics.

Approaching traffic

Principal work area

Movable display panel

Outside window

Equipment area

Secondary work area

ELLEN EDWARDS

Personalizing the work station. *Given an opportunity, most people will personalize their work stations.*

tant in work stations where personnel rotate. It is exceedingly unpleasant to come on duty at a toll station or a ticket counter and find that it has been left in a dirty, unsanitary condition.

PERSONAL STATUS

During the time an individual is at work, the character and quality of his or her work-station facilities becomes a measure of personal status, not only within the organization but to the world in general. Interpreting such symbols is not, however, easy and straightforward. The staff at corporate headquarters may work in superbly furnished and equipped surroundings. This does not necessarily reflect on the status of the individuals but rather on the image of the corporation. The true significance of such signs is seen in comparisons between individuals or groups of individuals. Individuals of equal rank or responsibility feel slighted if any of their peers within the organization receive better treatment, unless it results from an obvious functional requirement of their position. Employees who are dealing with credit matters, or personnel complaints, may reasonably be given private offices even though others in their salary brackets have to work in the open.

A designer's first concern is to provide facilities that employees view as being fair and just. There are other yardsticks that must be considered. If the legal secretaries in one law office conclude that their counterparts in most other offices are enjoying much better working conditions, they may feel slighted. Their sense of distributive justice, of their standing relative to others, is offended.

- **Involve people in the design process.** Including employees in the planning process is the best way of ensuring that they have work stations that fit their requirements while at the same time enlisting their support for the success of the project. In spite of the fears that are sometimes expressed by management, experience has indicated that when employees are involved in the planning process in a significant way, their suggestions are intelligent, relevant, and reasonable.

- **Appearance is important.** The appearance of the workplace, any workplace, is important to employees. The distinction that is sometimes drawn between public areas of an operation and behind-the-scenes areas where appearance does not count is unfair to the employees. It communicates the message that employees are less worthy of concern than the public. Regardless of the realities, no one likes that message.

- **Distribute amenities fairly.** Whatever resources are available should be distributed fairly. This does not mean that everyone should receive the same treatment. Differences in rank and responsibility are normal and so are differences in facilities and prerogatives. What offends the sense of fairness is obvious imbalance, where a disproportionate share of resources are devoted to a small group of people.

- **Stay within the norms of the field.** Be certain that the facilities are not notably inferior to those normally provided in the same field. If they are notably *superior* to the field there will be no complaint from the employees. They may, in fact, reduce employee turnover.

TERRITORIALITY

Territorial matters are discussed in more detail in the next section. The important consideration for the individual work station is boundaries.

- **Establish clear boundaries.** Any individual work station, one that is not shared, should be clearly bounded in a manner that is obvious to the user and to any neighbor who might otherwise intrude.

SHARED WORKPLACES

When personal workplaces are combined into shared workplaces, personal and social problems develop. The solitary worker avoids a number of problems that can occur when people work together. It is equally true that the solitary worker loses the comradeship of joint effort and the increased efficiency of cooperation and specialization. While certain activities require uninterrupted concentration that can probably be done best in solitary circumstances, there are many more that require close cooperation and face-to-face interaction between groups of people. These are the activities that are responsible for the ever larger concentrations of workers found in public agencies and private corporations.

Personal Space and *Personal Status* have been discussed previously in relation to *THE PERSONAL WORKPLACE* and are essentially the same in relation to *SHARED WORKPLACES*. A shared workplace is, after all, a collection of personal workplaces. It is worth stressing, however, that involving the workers in the design process is just as important to the success of shared workplaces as it is in personal workplaces. There are, in addition, important factors that are unique to the shared workplace.

GROUP MEMBERSHIP

Most working groups are assembled as a result of managerial decisions. They are not, in other words, self-selected social groups. As a result they do not fit exactly into the category of social groups discussed in Chapter 3. These chance groups do, however, exhibit normal preferences in regard to group size: They much prefer to work in smaller rather than larger groups. It has not been possible to find a specific number for an optimum working group and there probably is nothing fixed in this regard, but the preference is clear in relative terms.

It would also be helpful if a definitive statement could be made about the relative virtues of open-office planning or "office landscape" versus more conventional office arrangements. While many studies on this topic have been conducted, they are not conclusive. The preponderance of the evidence indicates that most office workers prefer conventional office layouts to open office spaces. Workers who have moved from conventional to open-plan offices feel that their efficiency is reduced and that they tend to cooperate less with their co-workers. Some studies, however, claim to find a high degree of satisfaction with open planning. This disparity may result from differences in research design. It could also indicate that other, more fundamental, factors are involved and that open planning that dealt with these factors would be as acceptable as more conventional arrangements.

- **Establish clear boundaries for working groups.** While this is a territorial recommendation, it appears here because it is an important part of establishing that there is, in fact, a group. The minimum requirement for defining boundaries is not clear. Ceiling-high partitions surrounding a space clearly accomplish this purpose. Whether lower partitions or partial enclosures accomplish this is open to question. It is likely that something less than complete physical separation is acceptable *as long as the occupants perceive it as complete*. This would require both visual and acoustic separation.

- **Keep working groups small.** Defining the size of a working team is generally a management prerogative. A designer seldom makes such decisions. A designer can, however, indicate the importance of subdividing large groups into smaller sections. While there are no specific guidelines on this point, studies on the nature of social groups indicate that groups of more than eight people find it difficult to focus on a common topic and tend to break into smaller groups. Social groups are not working groups, however, so this number is not precisely relevant. The best evidence available suggests that working teams of up to 12 are effective and groups as large as 35 are acceptable. A workable strategy would attempt to keep most groups close to 12 and establish a maximum upper limit of 35.

Morale always includes consensus on goals or values. The larger a group, the less probable it is that they will achieve consensus and hence higher morale.

■ **Concentrate entering traffic.** The traffic entering the area assigned to a group should be focused at a single major entry point.

■ **Provide an obvious focal point for the group.** An information or communication center should be provided at some point that is central to the group area or adjacent to an entrance to the group area. This may be as simple as a small bulletin board where group invitations, announcements, vacation schedules, ride exchanges, cartoons, and postcards from vacationing staff members can be displayed.

■ **Arrange space so the group can assemble.** The best way for a group of people to coordinate their activities and to understand their common objectives is to meet together. Make it possible for the group to gather within their own space for this purpose. This is not a formal assembly area but some part of the floor area where furniture can be shifted temporarily to permit a gathering.

■ **Any group space should have outside windows.** In spite of some studies that suggest that windows are not necessary, the preponderance of evidence indicates that most people prefer to work in places with windows and, furthermore, select locations close to windows in preference to any other locations.

■ **Protect the group space from distracting noise.** Obvious noise sources within the space should be controlled. Noisy equipment should be enclosed in acoustic hoods. The most troublesome noise sources, however, are those originating

Divide large departments into smaller sections.

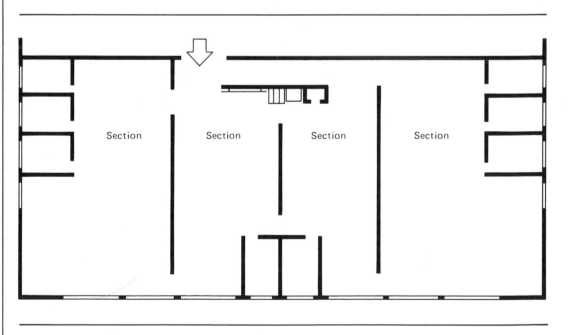

Provide a departmental information center.

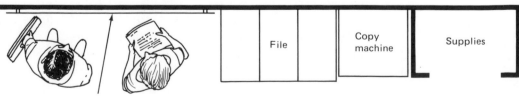

Bulletin board

outside the space. Of these, the most distracting are the sounds made by other people, especially other people talking.

- **Provide local control for mechanical and electrical systems.** The preceding section on *THE PERSONAL WORKPLACE* described the importance of giving each individual control over his or her personal lighting and comfort systems. If this should be an impossible goal, then at least provide controls within the group space. Totally automated systems that are completely beyond the control of the individuals involved are very frustrating.

THE PRIVATE OFFICE

The private workplace, whether it is office, laboratory, studio, or shop, has connotations of separateness or status that make it especially attractive. The private office is certainly perceived as a symbol of rank. While some private offices go with tasks that require confidentiality such as credit work, or creative problem solving such as computer programming, the majority of private offices reflect preference rather than necessity. It is probable that status has a lot to do with this preference, but a more basic factor is the strong desire expressed by most people to exercise control over their immediate environment and to control access to themselves. If American office workers were given the option of working in separate private spaces rather than in shared spaces, it is likely that there would be many more private offices than there are today.

While private offices have some characteristics that make them popular, they are not necessarily the most efficient arrangement for activities requiring a high degree of involvement with other people. It is hard to imagine that floor traders on stock or commodity exchanges could execute their high-speed transactions with equal efficiency if each were enclosed in a private office. There is no commu-

Provide an informal departmental assembly area.

nication technology now available or foreseeable that can quite equal the speed and efficiency of face-to-face transactions. We can imagine, however, that after the exchange is closed those same traders would prefer the privacy of a separate office for discussing sensitive business matters or concentrating on long-range planning.

Floor traders are not alone in their special needs. It appears that there are three categories of work situations rather than the two that are usually assumed: work that can be effectively done in a shared workplace, work that requires a private workplace, and work that requires both. The existence of this third category is not widely recognized and is seldom reflected in office layouts.

Assuming that a private workplace or office is required either because of privacy needs or as a symbol of rank, there are certain criteria it should meet.

PERSONAL SPACE

Given the need to conduct certain operations in private and the desire to control access, the only kind of office that fully satisfies those requirements is one that is actually private. Shared offices, open-front offices, glass-front offices, and offices surrounded by low partitions do not qualify. Complete acoustic and visual privacy is required and, somewhat surprisingly, acoustic isolation seems to be the more important of the two. Telephone conversations and people talking are more distracting than air-conditioning noise because we are more intertested in other people than we are in mechanical equipment.

- **Ensure visual privacy.** Provide ceiling-high walls and solid doors. If glass is used, provide shutters that can be closed when needed. A wide door or double doors make it possible for the office occupant to open the office to some extent.
- **Ensure acoustic privacy.** Ceiling-high walls and solid doors do not, in themselves, ensure acoustic privacy. Distracting noise leaks through air-conditioning ducts, electrical outlet boxes, under doors, and through the ceiling above the partitions. It is true that conversations are sometimes masked by the prevailing ambient noise level, but it is unwise to rely on such masking for privacy. A dead silence could be embarrassing.

Many of the other characteristics of the private office are shared with the personal workspace. These are discussed more fully in *THE PERSONAL WORKPLACE* section. Refer to that section for additional information on the recommendations listed below.

- **Identify the individual's office.** Provide a place for name and title.
- **Provide lockable personal storage.** Individuals should be able to lock their own offices. If this is not possible, at least provide a lockable cabinet or closet for them.
- **Face incoming traffic.** Make it possible for the occupants to arrange furnishings so that they can face incoming traffic.
- **Provide local control over light and heat.** The private office, particularly if used for small conferences, has a special need for individual environmental controls.
- **Provide flexible furnishings.** Give the occupants some options for arranging their furnishings to suit their individual work habits.
- **Provide for personalization.** Give the occupants some options for displaying personal items in their offices.

PERSONAL STATUS

This is an important consideration in designing any workplace, but it is especially important in the private office. Real or imagined disparities between the offices that are provided for individuals who believe that they have equal responsibilities and authority may result in feelings of distributive injustice. The insistence of

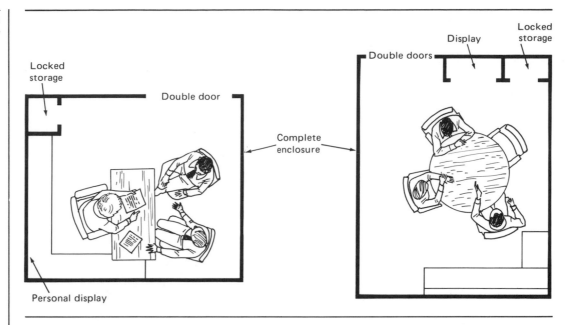

many corporations and public agencies on precisely matched accommodations for personnel at each rank is well founded. This equality, however, relates to the facilities provided by the employer. It does not need to interfere with the right of any individual to personalize a private office.

Recommendations previously made for *THE PERSONAL WORKPLACE* generally apply to offices as well.

- **Involve the occupants.** Whenever possible, the designer should involve the future occupants in planning their own offices.
- **Appearance is important.** The appearance of the workplace is an important matter to all employees. While some workers would be much easier to satisfy than others with regard to the character or quality of their physical surroundings, it is a rare individual who does not care about such things.
- **Distribute amenities fairly.** While some individuals are easier to satisfy than others insofar as their requests or requirements are concerned, this does not mean that they would happily accept less than their peers receive. Space, equipment, furnishings, and locations must be distributed fairly. This does not necessarily mean evenly. What is disturbing to the sense of distributive justice is being treated unfairly in comparison to one's peers or feeling that there has been a grossly unbalanced distribution of rewards.
- **Stay within the norms of the field.** While workers are most conscious of the benefits and perquisites awarded to their immediate peers in their own organization, they are also quite aware of what their peers in other organizations receive. While absolute parity in space, equipment, location, and furnishings is not required, there should be no glaring disparity in regard to these amenities.

TERRITORIALITY

Other than the requirement for privacy that can only be satisfied by having a separate, enclosed workplace, the principal reason for the private office is to satisfy the sense of territoriality. The private office is bounded by solid walls, the least ambiguous of territorial boundaries. It permits an almost complete degree of control over personal access and, because of its walls, is much more amenable to some degree of personalization than an open workplace. Since these characteristics have great appeal for many people it is not hard to understand why private offices are popular.

6 | MEETING TOGETHER

"Getting together" is one of the most human of human habits. While modern communications techniques have advanced to the point where information can be interchanged over great distances with speed and accuracy, that has not eliminated the need to get together for face-to-face meetings. To the degree that modern communication systems generate additional social and business activity, they increase rather than decrease the need for meeting face to face.

The attractions of face-to-face meetings are substantial. Face-to-face communications are more efficient than any written or electronic alternative. Not only can gestures, expressions, posture, and intonation be used to supplement words, but clarifications and amplifications can also be sought to confirm precise understanding. Such meetings give us the chance to raise those "Do you mean that . . ." or "But what if . . ." questions that are so important in helping us develop a full understanding of any information.

The ability to raise questions makes the face-to-face meeting especially useful in coordinating and motivating groups of people, exchanging ideas, and arriving at a consensus. The widespread acceptance of the practical value of group meetings is reflected in the innumerable conference rooms, committee rooms, seminar rooms, and assembly rooms that dot the territory of corporate, legislative, and academic America. Unfortunately, there is no corresponding evidence recognizing the equally valuable informal, spontaneous, meetings that occur in corridors, stair halls, coffee shops, lounges, waiting rooms, and lobbies, or outside on street corners and in parks. There is hardly a place where people meet that may not become the temporary setting for a meeting, though that fact is rarely reflected in the design of such places.

The logic behind this disparity is that meetings called for the benefit of the organization or the institution are an essential part of operations and deserve special spaces, but that other meetings must necessarily be for the benefit or entertainment of the individuals involved and do not deserve special recognition. This is only partially true. While certain informal, unscheduled gatherings are motivated solely by social interests, there are others that are highly productive both for the individuals involved and their organizations.

The tendency for high school and college students to gather at a favored beach is socially motivated. So is the gathering of their parents after work at the neighborhood tavern or in the bar at the club. However, the knots of students standing in the hallway or sitting on the school lawn discuss school work as well as social activities. The hurried discussions that occur in an office doorway serve to solve problems in a much more efficient way than calling a meeting. The casual encounters over a cup of coffee in the faculty lounge can resolve coordination problems that would be difficult to accomplish with memos.

The viewpoint advanced here is that it makes little difference whether meetings serve a functional purpose for an organization or institution, or whether they are solely intended for the entertainment of the individuals involved. In either case, they deserve to be supported by the design of the meeting place.

CONFERENCE ROOMS

The term "conference" is applied to meetings of all shapes and sizes. They may range from a group of three executives "conferring" on a departmental budget to an international gathering with a cast of thousands meeting to discuss some global problem. Since international gatherings, with their exotic problems of simultaneous translations, protocol, and precedence, are relatively rare, this section is focused on normal, or garden variety, conferences that are a staple of American life.

Communication is the principal purpose of a conference. It may also serve some secondary purposes, such as permitting the individuals who have been brought together for the meeting to resolve some unrelated problems of their own. This is possible because most meetings consist of three phases: the pre-meeting gathering, the meeting itself, and the post-meeting gathering. To function effectively, a conference room must satisfy all these needs. This is not difficult to do. A designer can, with relatively little effort, create a conference room that is extremely effective in satisfying these needs. There is nothing a designer can do, however, to ensure that a meeting will be effectively organized and led. As a consequence, there is no hope that we will ever see the end of boring, frustrating, time-wasting meetings.

COMMUNICATIONS

The term "conference" implies a gathering in which everyone is potentially a participant, in contrast to a "lecture" where there is a speaker and a relatively passive audience. If each individual is to be able to communicate effectively with every other individual, there are certain requirements that must be met.

- **Every participant can see the face of every other participant.** Reading facial expression is an important part of personal communications.
- **Every participant can face any speaker.**
- **Every participant can hear any speaker.**
- **Every participant can face any visual presentation.**

No configuration completely satisfies all these conditions. If there is no need for visual presentations that must be visible to everyone, then a circle becomes an ideal arrangement. If visual presentations are required, then a horseshoe-shaped arrangement comes closest to satisfying all the requirements.

Communication efficiency is greatly affected by distance. People who work together and are familiar with one another will normally elect a distance, from head

Effective conference configurations.

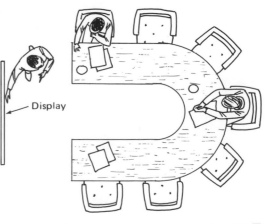

Display

to head, of from 4 to 7 feet for conversing. This would be the kind of group that might assemble in a private office around a desk.

Larger groups, assembled at a regular conference table, inevitably adopt a greater head-to-head distance. Assuming that each participant is allocated from 2½ to 3 feet of space at the table for manipulating papers and reports, note that:

■ **A circular table 6 feet in diameter can accommodate 6 or 7 people for a working conference.** This puts the group at a normal head spacing of about 7 feet. A table this size will only accommodate the stated number of people comfortably if the legs are properly located.

■ **A circular table 10 feet in diameter can accommodate 10 to 12 people for a working conference.** This puts the group at a normal head spacing of about 12 feet. At this size, it begins to be difficult to keep the attention of all participants focused on a common topic but communication remains efficient.

The circle can continue to be enlarged to accommodate more people, but beyond 10 feet communication becomes more formal and more difficult. Voices must be raised and gestures and facial expressions made more emphatic if they are to be heard and seen.

■ **If conference arrangements create head-to-head spacings greater than 20 feet, some form of voice amplification will normally be required** if everyone is to hear and comprehend a discussion accurately.

It is not always possible to accommodate large circular arrangements. If the shape is altered, made longer and narrower, the distance between individuals at the end of the table is increased and communication efficiency is reduced. In this case the 20-foot limitation is especially important.

When the number of conferees exceeds 20, it becomes more effective to provide a second row of seats rather than to continue to expand the table. This configuration obviously violates the requirement that every participant must be able to see the face of every other participant. The people on the same side of the table cannot see each other. The people in the second row cannot see much of anything, in fact, and are liable to lose interest in the proceedings if everyone is on the same level. This leads to a new requirement:

■ **In accommodating large groups where more than one row of seats is required, the additional rows of seats should be elevated.** This arrangement makes it possible for those participants in the elevated rows to both see and be seen by a large percentage of those present. They can feel that they are part of the group rather than an audience.

Small group discussion.

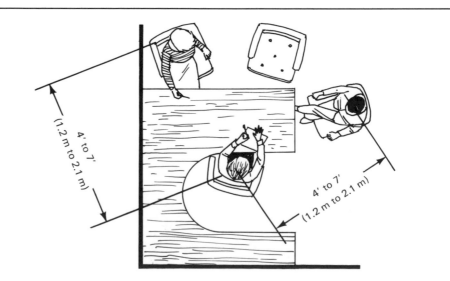

4' to 7'
(1.2 m to 2.1 m)

4' to 7'
(1.2 m to 2.1 m)

Screen

Lectern

20' (6 m) head spacing

In this large conference room, elevated seats for the staff and public make it possible for everyone to observe the activities at the main table.

A conference room should provide an area for pre- and post-meeting gatherings.

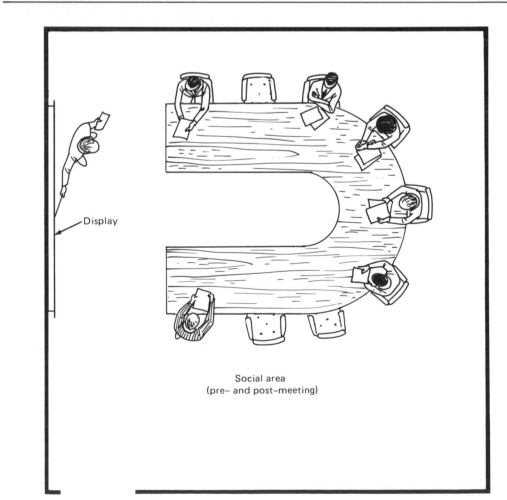

Display

Social area
(pre- and post-meeting)

When a group meeting can normally be expected to refer to visual and verbal presentations during the course of a meeting, such as film, slides, displays, and demonstrations, then the closed circle arrangements previously shown do not work well. If people who are seated in a closed circle must turn their common attention to a display or presentation, then some will have to shift away from the table to make this possible. Simply turning their chairs around will not provide a clear view for those behind them.

- **Where visual presentations and displays are a normal part of meeting agenda, a horseshoe configuration is more effective than a circle.**

For face-to-face communications to be as effective as possible, certain ambient conditions must be met. Lighting must be arranged so that faces and facial expressions can be clearly perceived; illuminating working and display surfaces is not enough. In face-to-face meetings, it is the face-to-face that counts and it is facial illumination that must be considered first.

Ambient acoustic conditions are another important factor in effective personal communications. Extraneous noises must be excluded from the meeting room, and room acoustics must be designed to favor the frequency range of human speech.

- **Illuminate the faces of those meeting with shadowless light so that they are seen against a nonglaring background.**
- **Provide a quiet meeting space, free of distracting noise, with room acoustics that favor the frequency range of the human voice.** One of the most distracting of all noises during a productive conference is the sound of a telephone ringing followed closely by the sound of someone talking on the telephone. Telephones should be kept out of conference rooms.

The fact that a group of people may have been assembled for a specific purpose does not deter them from using the occasion for purposes of their own. In any meeting, the participants begin to assemble shortly before the meeting begins; after the meeting there is a breakup period as members of the group drift away. During the pre-meeting and post-meeting phases, useful discussions can be held if there is space for such activities to take place.

- **Any meeting space should provide a standing area** that will accommmodate at least half of the people who are expected to attend during pre-meeting and post-meeting gatherings.

INFORMAL MEETING AREAS

Many meetings are scheduled, or occur spontaneously, in areas that were never intended for such use. Many churches, synagogues, public schools, and public libraries permit, or even encourage, community groups to use their facilities for public meetings. The section chief in some corporate department, or an equivalent official in a public agency, may choose to assemble the section personnel right in the office space where they work rather than move everyone to a conference room. Informal conferences of this kind are discussed in several other chapters.

It would be unwise from a functional standpoint to compromise the layout of a church, classroom, or office to accommodate such meetings. However, a designer should be conscious of the fact that they may occur and, further, that it may be very much to the benefit of the institution or organization providing the space to have them occur. Under these circumstances, making these spaces useful for meeting purposes should become a secondary part of the design problem.

This problem is frequently dealt with simply by turning the available space over to the users and letting them make out as well as they can. This is no solution at all. Given the normal configuration people adopt when they are conversing, if a space is to be useful for meeting purposes, it must accommodate something approaching a circle. A designer should test any floor-plan layout for its ability to accept a rearrangement that is appropriate for meetings. The layout should have the same basic characteristics as any conference room, modified by the practical necessity of fitting them into spaces that are intended primarily for other uses:

- **Keep the group within "social distance."** Provide a meeting area that will accommodate a 12-foot diameter circle.
- **Seating, tables, and other equipment that may be used should be easy to move.**
- **Lighting should be adaptable for meeting use.**
- **Sound control and acoustics should be appropriate for meeting purposes.**

PUBLIC PERFORMANCES

Public performances differ from the other types of assembly that we have discussed because they presume facilities for an audience. This distinction still covers a diverse array of events. They range in size from popular music extravaganzas with an audience measured in tens of thousands to amateur band concerts with more performers than listeners. Some offer mimes and comics, others offer lectures, debates, or panel discussions. Access is by reserved seating in some cases but in other cases is open to anyone willing to sit on the floor. The surroundings range from the grandeur of a metropolitan opera house to the worn simplicity of the local parish hall.

This section deals with a limited portion of the diverse array of public performances. Specifically, it covers those events where entertainers or lecturers perform before an audience at a scheduled time and place in a setting that is designed to accommodate such performances. Seats may be reserved and tickets sold, or the event may be open to the public without charge. A great deal of technical lore is available on such problems as sight lines, floor slopes, lighting, seat spacing, aisle widths, and the techniques of scenery and set management. None of these is discussed here. This section deals only with the behavioral aspects of such performances from the standpoint of the performers and the individuals in the audience.

PERSONAL STATUS

The paramount concern in designing any room or hall for public performances is to make it possible for the audience to see without obstructions and to hear clearly what the performers have to offer. No other considerations can be permitted to interfere with this requirement. If anything does interfere with the ability to see and hear clearly, the audience will feel that their legitimate interests have been ignored and will feel some resentment toward those who are responsible for the problem.

Performers are also sensitive to slights on their personal worth or merit. Professional concert artists would hardly expect the high-school gymnasium to have excellent acoustics, or to find well-equipped dressing rooms there. They do have a right to expect, however, that a real effort has been made to organize the audience so that they could both see and hear, to place the audience so that the performers could address them directly, and to provide whatever facilities and equipment the performers must have to perform well. If the performers are put in a position where they cannot perform well, the implication is that their performance is not worthy of better treatment. This is true for lectures and demonstrations as well as entertainment.

- **For audiences, the right to see and hear well is paramount.**
- **For performers, the right to have an audience that can see and hear well is paramount.**

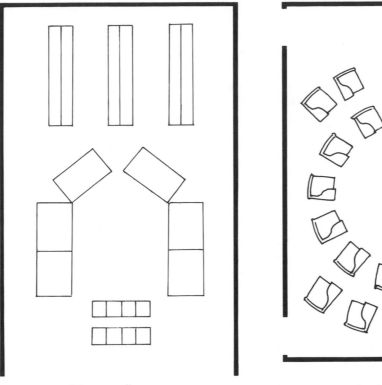

Library reading room   Academic classroom

Meeting in a public library.

CUE SEARCHING

People approach many public performances in a tentative, uncommitted way. They study the displays in the theater lobby, listen to the sideshow barkers at the county fair, or stand in the doorway of the student lounge to see if the speaker has anything important to say. In effect they are weighing the cost to them in time and money versus the benefits offered by the performance. Where events are highly advertised and admission is by ticket only, this browsing or shopping behavior is minimized. Where events are open to the public without charge, and where other options are offered at the same time, this behavior is intensified. It can be seen frequently at fair grounds and is commonplace on college campuses.

If we assume that any performance has some merit for someone, then it would be in the best interest of the public as well as the performers if the maximum number of people were aware of the program and its content. The design of the approach to the performance area has a bearing on this point.

■ **The approach to a performance area should provide for displays that describe the performance in some detail.**

■ **The performance area should be openable to the extent that the potential audience can sample the performance.** Obviously the performance area would have to be closed for events where tickets have been sold.

Performance-area characteristics.

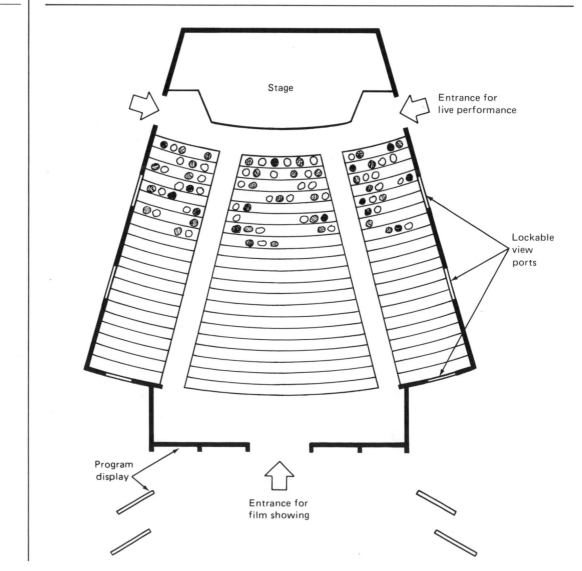

COMMUNICATIONS

Any kind of performance is an act of communication involving a sender, a message, and a receiver. The content of the message may be largely emotional, as in a concert, or largely intellectual, as in a lecture. In any case the communication requirements remain the same. (See *Communications* section, Chapter 3.)

Communication requires visibility and audibility and is greatly affected by distance. As a consequence, both sender and receiver, performer and audience, benefit if they can be close together. The immediacy and effectiveness of communication is greatly enhanced when the performer draws close to the audience. There are obviously practical limits to this general rule: Members of the audience can enjoy being a lot closer to a lecturer, or nightclub comedian, than they can to the high-school marching band.

The tendency of people to approach an event in a tentative fashion, reserving final judgment and protecting their escape routes, often creates a dispersed audience that is not in close contact with the performer. The audience tends to select seats near the entrances and along the aisles first, rather than assembling in a group close to the performers.

To improve communication between audience and performers, a designer should strive to meet the following requirements.

■ **Project the performer or performers into the audience.** There are obvious practical limits to this requirement. There may have to be compromises between the needs of different programs and different groups. Nevertheless, the importance of bringing performers and audiences close must not be underestimated.

■ **Locate the entrances close to the stage or performing area.** This entrance location will have the effect of concentrating the audience near the stage rather than dispersing it along the aisles. Without suggesting that a church service is in any way like a performance, this same entrance arrangement in a church will give the minister a chance to greet the parishioners as they file out.

OPEN ASSEMBLY

A variety of events are staged, or occur, in public spaces that are not normally regarded as assembly areas. These can be found in parks and playgrounds, on schoolgrounds and college campuses, in shopping malls, and in the streets and plazas of the city. They include football rallies, political demonstrations, Christmas programs, and Salvation Army Band concerts. They include public ceremonies (such as the celebration of Veterans Day), break-dancing demonstrations in the park, and two musicians sitting on the grass who have attracted a small group of listeners.

While many events of this type are scheduled and conducted with the approval of whatever agency controls the space, others are spontaneous. Some of the spontaneous activities are not exactly welcome in some circumstances; nevertheless, this class of activity embraces many legitimate reasons for groups to assemble, and they should be accommodated.

Fortunately, there are physical characteristics that tend to generate such gatherings and other characteristics that tend to discourage them. A designer thus has some measure of influence over the kind of events that take place and the location where they occur.

CUE SEARCHING

As people move along a public way they will perceive their environment, and react to it, in one of two ways: in an habitual mode or in an exploratory mode. Those who are familiar with an area move with confidence and pay little obvious attention to their surroundings. Those who are new to an area, and are exploring it for the first time, are more tentative in their movements and are much more attentive to their surroundings. Both habitual and exploratory movement can be observed in the business district of any community that attracts even a small number of visitors. They can also be observed in the entrance lobbies of public buildings, museums, shopping malls, or any other structures that attract people who have never been there before. The habitués move ahead with confidence; the newcomers move slowly and search continuously for cues.

People who are moving in an exploratory mode are obviously looking for cues, while people who are moving in an habitual mode do not appear to be interested in cues at all. This is misleading. The habitués are simply more selective. While

Locate open-assembly event sites at traffic concentrations.

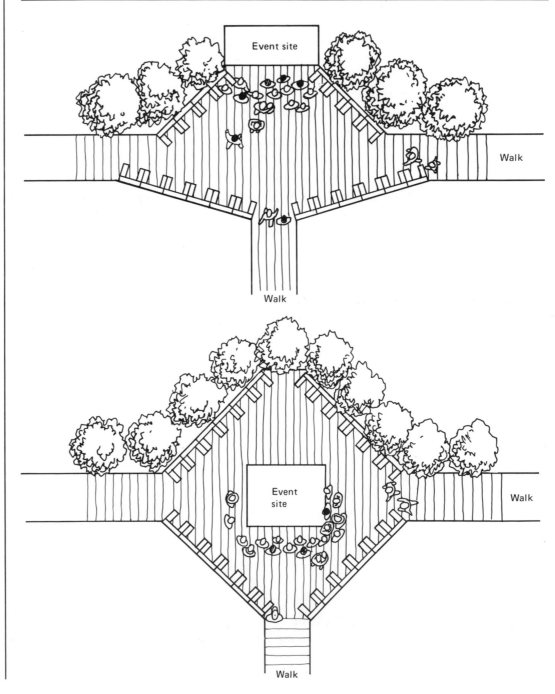

they seem to be oblivious to their surroundings, they can respond quickly to stimuli that hold some interest for them, such as headlines, friends, merchandise displays, or activities. This results largely from "incident hunger"—the need to inform themselves about what is going on in the world about them.

The characteristic search for cues can be of great value to a designer. By locating event sites at those points where cues can be picked up most readily by passing traffic, they can ensure that the sites will be utilized most effectively.

- **Locate event sites at a traffic crossroads or adjacent to a traffic stream.**
- **Arrange the event site so that any activity will be readily apparent to passing traffic.**
- **Provide a space where an audience can stand to sample a performance.**
- **Provide a place where an audience can sit to watch a performance.**

Open-assembly sites can also be located at interior traffic concentrations, as in shopping malls or in this student union building.

These requirements may seem self-evident, but many performance and assembly areas in shopping malls, public parks, and college campuses have been located without regard for them and, as a result, are much less useful and effective than they should be.

COMMUNICATIONS

Communication requirements for meetings and performances have been discussed earlier in this chapter and do not change for open assemblies. There are some unique problems, however, that can arise to restrict the usefulness of open-assembly areas. The principal problem has to do with scale. A small group that occupies a large assembly area effectively forestalls any other users. The same area divided or separated into smaller assembly areas can support a larger number of activities and enhance the diversity and the options available to the public. While exact sizes cannot be given, the general rule is clear.

■ **A number of smaller assembly areas will be more useful than a single large area.** As a rough guideline, four areas in a public park that might each attract and accommodate 100 people would be more useful than having only one area that might accommodate 400 people.

7 SHOPPING TOGETHER

Shopping, which includes bartering and buying both the luxuries and necessities of life, is another aspect of human life that is nearly universal. It is for most people a necessity, for others a pleasure, and for some a hobby.

The factors that motivate an individual to acquire a specific item are inherent in the individual and in the item acquired. The considerations that lead a shopper to select one sweater over another, or to pick up one box of laundry detergent rather than another, are not matters that a designer of shops and shopping centers can influence. There are aspects of shopping behavior that are, however, of great importance to designers, since these aspects are affected by the location of the store and the physical characteristics it displays to the shopping public.

Shoppers can be categorized in an infinite number of ways. For our purposes we will divide them into four sets.

- **Shoppers who are satisfying an immediate need.** This is the kind of shopping that is done when people stop at the local convenience store on the way home to buy a frozen dinner or go out Sunday morning to buy the newspaper. For those who are shopping in this manner, convenience and time saving are the important factors in deciding where to shop and what selection to make.
- **Shoppers who are making routine purchases of household necessities.** This would include everything from weekly grocery shopping to buying back-to-school clothes for children. In this kind of shopping, convenience is important but price is a controlling factor.
- **Shoppers who are making infrequent purchases of lasting items.** Shopping for household appliances and furnishings falls within this category. A wide selection and a choice of sources are important. Price is also important, but convenience is no longer a major concern.
- **Shoppers who regard the act of shopping as a shared recreational or social event.** In this case the unique quality of the merchandise and the unique quality of the shopping environment become very important. This does not necessarily imply a unique architectural environment. Swap meets and farmers markets may meet the above criteria as well as high-fashion shopping centers.

Shopping is such a commonplace activity and goes on so frequently in so many places, that it is difficult to deal with it in terms of specific locations. The recommendations that follow are focused on those characteristics of shopping places that will motivate shoppers. These recommendations apply to some degree to the sidewalk vendor of soft pretzels as well as the sophisticated merchants of the suburban shopping mall—but not equally.

Recreational shopping can be anything out of the ordinary.

A PLACE TO SHOP

The choice of a place to shop is influenced by the nature of the purchase and the current needs and preferences of the shopper. Depending on our concerns of the moment, any of us could fall into any of the four shopping categories described previously. Regardless of our mood or needs of the moment, we can only select a place to shop based on the information that is made available to us. Most communication of a commercial nature has moved from the marketplace to the media. Radio, television, and the print media have largely taken over the job of getting the customers into the store, largely but not completely. The layout and design of a store still have an important role to play in motivating the customers. This is accomplished when the information communicated by the design satisfies the shopper's needs or interests of the moment.

COMMUNICATIONS

In Chapter 3, in the section on *Communications*, there is a brief list of essential information that any building should impart to an interested viewer:

- What is it?
- What benefit does it offer me?
- How do I get in?
- What is inside?
- How will I be received?

Answering these questions is an important function of the design of a shopping area. From the designer's point of view it becomes imperative that the target group of customers be accurately identified, that the design create an image of the establishment that is clear and understandable to these customers, and that every aspect of the project be used to support this image. The nature of the factors to be stressed will depend on the nature of the establishment and the customers it hopes to attract.

- **Define the customer group that is sought and the characteristics that are important to them.** This, of course, is a process of defining the objectives of the project in human terms—a fundamental first step in any design program.
- **Answer the five basic questions clearly and effectively.**
  1. *What is it?* This question generally is answered by means of signs, but the designer should use any other semantic means available to reinforce the message.
  2. *What benefit does it offer me?* This question is also answered by means of signs, but displays of materials and merchandise become very important in providing explicit, detailed answers.
  3. *How do I get in?* Signs are useful, sometimes essential, in responding to this question, but symbols are often better. A visible parking lot, with empty spaces visible, communicates a message more effectively than a sign saying "Parking Lot." Visible pylons or gateposts fix the location of a parking lot entrance better than a sign or an arrow.

     A store that will serve pedestrian traffic on a suburban shopping street will not need a dramatically visible entrance to tell people where to enter. A shopping mall, however, seen across acres of parked cars should have a powerful architectural entrance feature to act as a landmark for people navigating across the blacktop.
  4. *What is inside?* Some enterprises may be so well known to their target audience that the name alone is enough to answer this question. Most enterprises will do better to make certain that shoppers can see for themselves what is

Chairs and tables identify this establishment even better than signs.

This menu display makes clear what this establishment offers and what it charges.

inside. "Window shopping" means just that; there must be some means for the shopper to evaluate what is offered and to compare it with other offerings.

5. *How will I be received?* This question cannot actually be answered through architectural means. What shoppers want to know is how they will be received by the people inside, a question no architect can possibly answer. The best a designer can do is to provide easy access, remove physical barriers, open the establishment for inspection, provide a comfortable and attractive interior, and let the shopping public decide for themselves if they will be properly received.

■ **Stress the design elements that will motivate the target population.** In this instance symbolism can communicate as effectively as words. This is where the designer's talent for communicating through design detail is challenged.

If convenience and timesaving are important, the location of the entrance must be clear and obvious. In many cases this means that the entrance to the parking lot, and the fact that parking spaces are available, must be emphasized. In some cases this requires that the parking lot be in front of the structure, or at least clearly visible to passersby.

If an establishment offers goods and services that are of high quality and therefore high priced, the materials used as well as the design, should reflect a similar quality. The important point is that as the design takes shape, each design element must be judged on the basis of its effect on the target group rather than solely on abstract esthetic merit.

PERSONAL STATUS

While people shop with different priorities at different times, this does not mean that they abandon any of their shopping preferences. The preferences are the same, only the ranking is altered. Shoppers in a hurry will not worry too much about price. If price is important, however, shoppers will put up with considerable inconvenience and indifferent service if they feel they are getting a bargain.

If two establishments offer equivalent bargains, the choice between them will be made on some basis other than price. Convenience may be the next factor taken into account, and the attitude of the personnel will be an important element. At some point, if all other factors are equal, the fact that one store has a more attractive ambience than another and thoughtfully provides for the comfort of its customers will provide the basis for choosing one source over another. These distinctions are not necessarily made as part of a conscious evaluation. They are seemingly made without thought, but the factors mentioned above form the basis for choice.

In any area where the marketplace is truly competitive, the store design and the effort made to provide for the comfort and convenience of the customers can be of critical importance. A designer should carefully think through the actions and needs of the various groups of people who may use the store and provide for them in the design. The kind of concern the designer should look for is illustrated by the following examples.

■ **Provide seating for people who must wait.** This starts outside the front door. It is common to find people waiting at the front door for an establishment to open for business. This is especially noticeable at banks and department stores. Benches at the front entrance would be a convenience for customers who arrive early and would be regarded as a thoughtful gesture by them.

When couples shop together there will be numerous instances where one is actively shopping and the other is waiting. Having a place to sit while waiting is especially attractive to older shoppers. While it is customary to find seating provided in many clothing stores, it is almost unheard of in hardware stores or supermarkets—yet the need is the same.

- **Provide for parcels.** Much shopping is done in concentrated forays where a number of establishments are visited in order to procure a number of different items. In the course of this activity it is normal to accumulate a variety of parcels. These become increasingly burdensome and difficult to handle, particularly when shoppers are looking at merchandise in other stores. Providing space or even keyed lockers where parcels and purse can be deposited while new purchases are made is another thoughtful provision.
- **Provide for children.** Parents with small children find it easier and more enjoyable to shop where the children will not be regarded as a nuisance, where it is unlikely that they will damage anything, and where there is some activity to occupy the children. Where these conditions are met, the parents are apt to be more attentive and receptive customers.

  Some stores go to great lengths to attract young families with children and to make special provisions for the children. Many others who should logically do the same thing ignore the problem completely. Merchants who handle big ticket items that typically require lengthy negotiations, such as appliance and automobile dealers, should give special thought to keeping the children occupied and out of their parents' hair while the negotiations are proceeding.
- **Provide for the elderly and the handicapped.** Any store anywhere should provide for the special needs of elderly and handicapped customers beyond the strict requirements of the law. In areas that may have a high percentage of elderly customers it becomes particularly important that these provisions be obvious. In addition to the usual requirements, automatic doors should be provided and the furnishings and equipment should be light enough to be easily shifted.

A PLACE TO EAT

For human beings, eating is an activity that is done sometimes in haste, sometimes at leisure, and sometimes with elaborate ceremony. People's eating habits at home are very personal and may range from the skimpiest kind of breakfast-on-the-run to festive banquets at Thanksgiving and Christmas. People's eating habits away from home are a great deal more like their shopping habits, and they are motivated to select one eating place over another on the basis of many of the same factors that influence their choice of shopping places.

Just as shoppers were classified into four categories, people who are shopping for a place to eat can be separated into four categories.

- **People who want to eat quickly.** Almost everyone fits into this category at some time: people who are late for an appointment or a class, people who have used up their lunch hour for shopping and need to get back to work, people who have only a few minutes before catching a plane or a bus. Convenience and time saving are the most important concerns for people in this group. Cost, service, and even the quality of the food are relatively unimportant.
- **People who want to eat well but informally.** Quality and service are important if they do not require formal dress or formal behavior. People who want to "eat out" but do not want to get dressed up fall into this category, as would those who are traveling with a carful of children.
- **People who savor excellent food.** Speed and convenience are relatively unimportant to this group. They are willing to spend the time and make the effort if the quality of the food and service are outstanding.

- **People who associate food and ceremony.** This group is looking for prestige as well as for something to eat. Most expense-account eating falls within this category. People who want to make eating a festive event, celebrate a birthday or anniversary, or entertain out-of-town visitors will seek this kind of eating place. The food may be outstanding, but that is not the crucial ingredient.

Eating is a social event in our society. In the home it is a family event. Outside the home it is a time when people gather with friends and acquaintances. Lunchtime may bring together a construction crew eating out of brown bags or business executives gathering at a downtown club. In either case the motivation is the same: to treat mealtime as a social event to be shared with friends and acquaintances. The social nature of mealtime has some special implications for the design of eating places, whether they are fashionable restaurants, employees' cafeterias, or dormitory dining rooms.

One obvious effect of the social nature of shared meals is the amount of time spent at the table. In a study conducted on a college campus, Robert Sommer found that solitary students averaged 15 minutes per meal, students with others of their own sex averaged 28 minutes per meal, and students with members of the opposite sex averaged 34 minutes per meal. While Sommer's study should not be extrapolated to predict eating times under other circumstances, it clearly demonstrates the social aspect of mealtime.

Wherever an eating establishment is located, there will be certain design characteristics that will affect the users.

COMMUNICATIONS

The communication characteristics previously discussed under the heading *A PLACE TO SHOP* generally apply to eating places and are not repeated here. As in any design project, the critical first step in designing an eating place is establishing its objectives; for commercial establishments that means defining with some precision the kind of customers sought. Once the customers are targeted, the establishment can be designed to cater to their special needs and preferences. The detailed design should communicate the answers to the questions posed earlier.

- What is it?
- What benefit does it offer me?
- How do I get in?
- What is inside?
- How will I be received?

There are several aspects of food-service shopping that are different from other forms of shopping. One of these differences has to do with sanitation. While it is hard to see how any business establishment in this country could be successful if it were not maintained in a neat and sanitary fashion, the public's general concern with this issue is magnified when it comes to food service. The actual sanitary conditions that prevail in an establishment are impossible for the public to measure. Presumably these are monitored by the public-health agencies. The public is, however, very conscious of the *impression* of cleanliness created by the design and the choice of materials.

- **The exterior and the interior of a food-service establishment must convey an image of immaculate cleanliness.** It is not enough to keep the premises clean. Trash- and waste-storage areas must be completely segregated and out of public view.
- **Eliminate food odors both inside and outside.** Some food odors are a magic stimulant to appetite; others are not. While an exception could certainly be made for popcorn vendors and bakeries, as a general rule it is safest to exhaust all kitchen air so that it cannot possibly be short-circuited back into the interior.

GROUP MEMBERSHIP

Since mealtime is closely tied to social activities, it should be natural for food-service establishments to recognize that fact in their layout and design. This is not always the case. Any eating place where management would like to attract patrons who regard mealtime as a social event should make some special provisions that reflect this concern. This is true whether it is a private club, a public restaurant, or a college dining hall.

■ **Provide an adequate waiting area.** A waiting area is not solely to accommodate overflow crowds that cannot be seated immediately; it is also to accommodate people who are waiting for friends to join them. It should be arranged and equipped to accommodate small groups of two or three who are waiting for the rest of their party to assemble.

■ **Provide an overview of the eating area from the waiting area.** In many circumstances, as in employee cafeterias, university dining halls, private clubs, and restaurants that become social centers, it is routine for individuals to join friends who are already seated if there is an empty seat. The process of locating both friends and empty seats is greatly facilitated if there is an overview of the eating area from the entry. This works best if the entry is slightly elevated.

■ **Provide a "stall" area between the entry and the eating area.** People entering an eating establishment normally slow down or stop, once inside, to evaluate their options. This is particularly true of new patrons but applies to all patrons to some extent. In cafeteria lines the stall area is found when the customer exits from the cafeteria line and begins to look for friends or a free seat.

■ **Provide tables that promote the desired social activities.** There are several different types of table-and-chair arrangements that encourage different types of groups.

1. If it is desirable to encourage people to feel free to join others by taking any open seat, round tables are most conducive to this practice.

2. If it is desirable to accommodate couples or groups who want some degree of privacy while eating, high-backed booths or high-backed winged chairs work best.

3. If it is desirable to accommodate loners who do *not* consider mealtime a social event, provide single tables.

In most instances it would be appropriate to satisfy all these different requirements by providing all these different types of seating. The important thing to remember is that no single arrangement of tables and chairs will be equally suitable for all types of users.

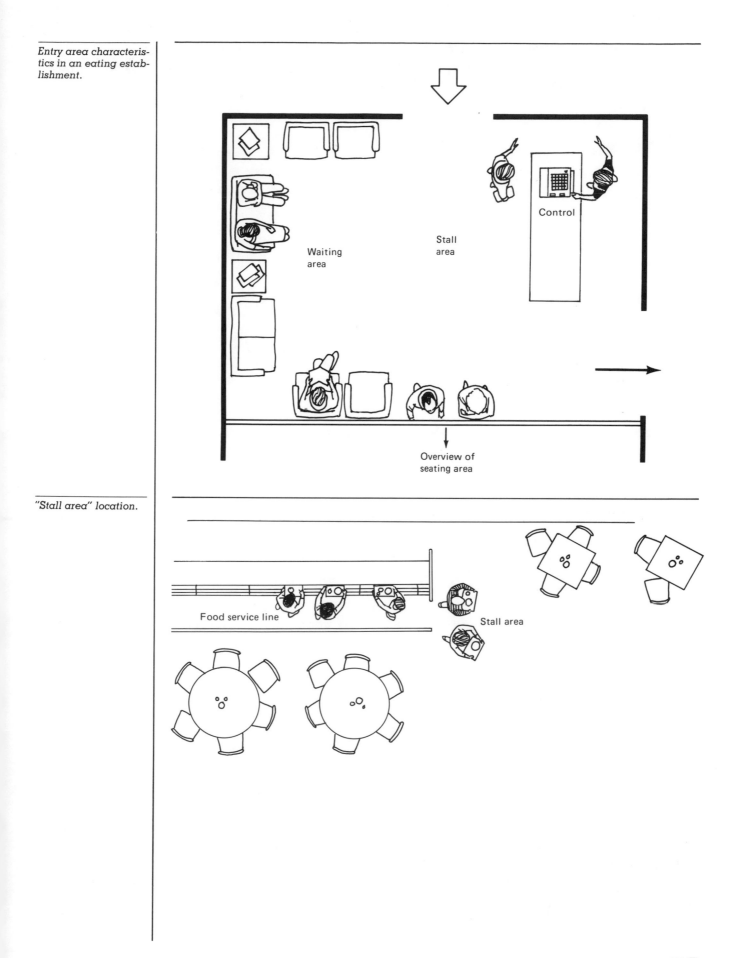

Entry area characteristics in an eating establishment.

Control

Stall area

Waiting area

Overview of seating area

"Stall area" location.

Food service line

Stall area

8 | LEARNING TOGETHER

Learning can be a lifelong process. While learning is usually thought of in terms of teachers and pupils in specially equipped places called classrooms, it is actually an activity that takes place whenever an individual responds knowingly to a stimulus. Learning means acquiring new knowledge, skills, and even wisdom. Consequently, it occurs anywhere a stimulus may be encountered: at work, at play, in the streets, and in the school corridors, as well as in classrooms.

Any setting has educational potential. When more than one person is present the potential is increased, since all people bring with them different experiences and different perceptions. Obviously, a designer working out the arrangements for classrooms, lecture halls, and teaching laboratories will try to employ all the available resources to expedite and enhance the learning experience. It is not nearly so obvious, however, that a designer could increase the educational potential of many other places simply by making certain that their nature or function is understandable to anyone who encounters them.

There are certain nonclassroom settings, such as museums, zoos, and parks displaying some natural phenomenon, where education is clearly a part of the basic mission. It would be rather unusual, however, for the layout of a wholesale produce terminal or the dispatch center of the local fire department to be considered as an educational opportunity. Nor is it often recognized that helping new employees, new customers, or new visitors understand the nature, purpose, and organization of the company they work for or the buildings they visit is an ever-recurring educational problem. This is a learning process that can be materially influenced by appropriate design features. Such opportunities should not be overlooked. Not many citizens get to City Hall nowadays, but if they do, it would be unfortunate if they failed to gain a clearer and more accurate grasp of how city government operates.

The stimuli or learning resources that may be provided vary greatly with the setting. In a classroom that is part of an organized school system, the resources seem boundless: There are instruments, training equipment, specimens, models, reference works, data banks, and trained guidance for using these sources to intensify the learning experience. In some of the other settings mentioned above, the resources may be nothing more than a sign, a display, a map, a commemorative plaque, or a vista. Whatever the level of stimulus, the ambient conditions must be suitable, with appropriate lighting, acoustics, ventilation, and a safe place to sit or stand in comfort in order to absorb the information.

THE SCHOOLGROUND OR CAMPUS

Any institution devoted to learning—whether it is elementary, middle school, high school, college, graduate or continuing education school—functions both as a learning center and a complex social organization. Wherever it is located, even on the upper floors of an urban office building, it has a "schoolground" or "campus."

There are corridors, foyers, stair halls, elevator lobbies, or other nonacademic spaces where students, and to some extent faculty, interact. These spaces should not be viewed as merely utilitarian adjuncts of the teaching spaces themselves. They are an integral part of the educational setting. Consequently, the school layout or campus plan must be designed to foster out-of-class learning just as the teaching stations must be designed to foster in-class learning.

GROUP MEMBERSHIP

The extent to which out-of-class learning experiences occur is related to the freedom and mobility of the students. At elementary levels, where students are normally kept together during the day, there is less interaction than there is in high school where students move between classes and are in contact with many

Learning can occur wherever there is a source of information.

more of their classmates. The opportunity for interaction is greatest on college and university campuses where students have the most freedom in allocating their time. Because of these differences, the recommendations that follow do not apply equally in all circumstances.

- **Keep school units small.** One of the most critical factors affecting students' feelings about their school, their involvement, and their sense of accomplishment is the size of the school. Studies have shown that students in smaller schools participated more in extracurricular activities, had a more positive self-image, showed a greater sense of responsibility, and were more sensitive to the needs of others. The data supporting this conclusion conform to the general principles discussed under the heading of *Group Membership* in Chapter 3.

  Unfortunately, there are no precise data on what constitutes the dividing line between "small" and "large." A college of two thousand students might be considered "small," but a grammar school of that size would usually be considered "large."

  One useful guideline for determining the size of a school is to limit it to the size necessary to accommodate a full range of academic offerings that are relevant to its principal mission. Beyond that point it would be wiser to create an additional unit than continually to expand the first unit.

- **Create informal social centers.** Students at all educational levels have a tendency to self-segregate themselves into groups and to identify themselves with specific spaces. This is not necessarily a territorial identification but simply a place where one is apt to find friends. These social centers exist whether we elect to provide them or not. A study made by Richard Myrick of high schools in the Washington, D.C., area identified these social centers and found that students checked through these centers several times a day. Myrick's study also found that much of the conversation that took place in the high-school corridors and on the lawn dealt with classes, studies, and school activities.

  It is not necessary to think of these informal social centers as lounges. They are more likely to be an area in the stair hall, a special tree on the lawn or the entrance steps. The spontaneous selection of these social centers may create problems that can be avoided if they are worked out in advance. A spontaneously generated social center at the building entrance can be a real impediment to traffic in and out. It is much better to plan for a social center *next* to the entrance with seats that are not hot in summer and cold in winter and that don't get wet when the lawn is sprinkled.

  The general characteristics of informal school social centers are:

  1. They must be on or adjacent to a major campus circulation route. Trying to shift an informal social center to some more remote spot will generally not work unless some compelling attraction is added to draw students away from their normal routes.
  2. They are most likely to be successful at a crossroads, at a major destination, or in conjunction with food services.
  3. They should provide some form of seating.
  4. They should provide some form of shelter.

- **Provide news and information centers.** In order to feel that you are a member of a group you must feel that you know what the group is doing and what it is concerned with. The location requirements for information centers are similar to the requirements for informal social centers. The two functions could easily coincide. If there is only one information center, it should be located at a major crossroad.

A *"spontaneously gen-
erated social center."*

*Locate informal social
areas so they will not
interfere with traffic at
building entrances.*

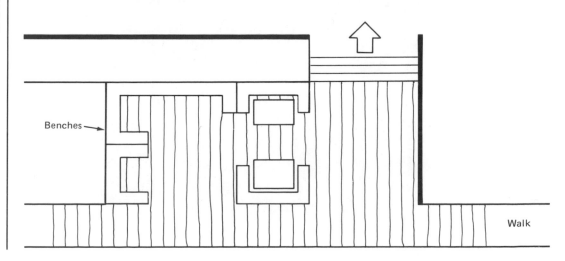

Benches →

Walk

A news and information center should be prepared to handle different types of information:

1. Communications from the institution to the student body.
2. Communications from organized groups, such as clubs, to the student body.
3. Communications from individuals to individuals. There must be some means for the campus community to arrange car pools and sell or trade surplus records, books, musical instruments, and athletic gear. Communications of this nature should be confined to a bulletin board that is clearly set apart from the boards reserved for official posters and announcements.
4. Graffiti: There is one other type of communication that might be included. Few individuals today have an opportunity to voice their opinions about the state of the world, or the state of the school, before an audience of their

An information center should bring together all the formal channels of communication.

peers. Consequently these opinions sometimes surface in socially unacceptable ways such as graffiti. The provision of panels for the free expression of opinion adds a great deal of interest to any information center.

Gossip, which is perhaps the most important, and surely the most prevalent, form of information exchange, does not require any special attention from the designer. It will take care of itself.

■ **Provide informal areas for solitary and group study.** Whenever students have time between classes, and their class situations demand it, they will use small amounts of free time for study wherever there is a convenient place. Observations on college campuses suggest that this studying frequently takes place at or near their classroom destination, sitting on the floor in the classroom corridors, on the building steps, or on the raised planters at the entrance.

A local bulletin board.

The design of this classroom corridor doesn't make any provision for the fact that students tend to study at their principal destinations.

A study area for students at a building entrance arranged for group study.

Informal study areas should be located at major academic destinations, either at the building entrance or in the corridors. They should provide seating with tables or tablet arms, and should be arranged so that groups can form and study together. Informal study areas should be acoustically separated from classrooms.

PERSONAL SPACE

While social interaction is an important part of school and should be recognized as such in school planning, that does not mean that individuals' preferences for places that are personally theirs is eliminated just because they are in school. Indeed, the need for some personal space is much harder to satisfy on most schoolgrounds and campuses than is the need for socializing. Many high schools provide lockers for each student so that there is at least a place to store books and equipment. Most colleges and universities do not even go that far. On nonresidential campuses, the college student's personal space may be a car or a backpack. It would be desirable if every student had a personal space, as suggested below, where he or she could exercise control.

■ **Provide each student with a lockable carrel or other personal space.** Each carrel should be equipped with a desk section for study and writing, an electrical outlet for typewriter or computer connection, an adjustable light, and storage for books, papers, and other student needs. It should be lockable and, above all, it should permit students to personalize the space as they wish.

A permanently assigned student carrel.

PERSONAL STATUS

The fact that schools accept new students in groups at specific times of the year, in a sort of batch system, inevitably leads to a certain amount of herding. The larger the institution, the more likely it will be that students will be dealt with in an impersonal fashion. Combined with the various forms of hazing that older students frequently practice on younger students, the system seems to demean incoming students systematically.

Treatment of this type will certainly affect the entering student's sense of self-esteem. While it is unlikely that designers will find a way to solve this problem, they may ameliorate the effects by providing new students with the same prerogatives and facilities as old students. If new students were provided with the same private, locked carrels as everyone else, they would at least feel less of a caste distinction.

CUE SEARCHING

School authorities recognize the problems that new students have in finding their way around a schoolground or campus. Indoctrination sessions and guided tours are frequently offered to minimize the newcomers' problems. Designers can contribute a great deal to making a campus more hospitable and understandable by providing appropriate signs, labels, maps, and landmarks.

It may seem wasteful to expend much effort in making a campus plan understandable, since all students will, of necessity, ultimately learn the system. What makes it important is the fact that newcomers are a constant on any schoolground. There is always a new crop. The following recommendations will make it easier for each new batch of students to learn their way around.

- **Create a plan with a clear, easily understood form.** Complexity has its place in architecture but not in the organization of a school site. If students can grasp the overall form, they can more easily plug their destinations into that framework.
- **Clearly name and number buildings.** This should be done so that names and numbers can be seen clearly from each point of approach.
- **Provide "you-are-here" maps at principal entry points.** (See the section on *Cue Searching* in Chapter 3.)
- **Provide visible landmarks.** We navigate through familiar terrain by unconsciously referring to landmarks, and we give directions to others by consciously referring to landmarks. We are seldom aware of our dependence on landmarks until we walk through a familiar area in a fog and experience a strange sense of being lost on our own home grounds.

    Landmarks are almost essential if "you-are-here" maps are to work well. They should be tall enough to be seen and unique enough to be remembered easily. A landmark may be a tree, a building, a flagpole, a fountain, a statue, a bell tower, a clock tower, or some feature not yet imagined.

    In any of those forms, a landmark that serves as a navigational aid may also, in time, become a campus symbol, a collective representation that binds alumni to the institution.

CLASSROOMS

Classrooms comprise a wide-ranging category that covers teaching–learning activities ranging from kindergartens to graduate seminar rooms, from workshops to gross-anatomy laboratories. Although some of these classrooms require highly specific features, in some ways they are quite similar. They all involve teaching, which, at its best, can be a marvelous demonstration of effective communication, but only if physical conditions make that possible.

COMMUNICATIONS

While the foundation of teaching is the ability to motivate people to want to learn, there must be an effective interchange between teacher and pupil before this can happen. Classroom design must therefore focus on providing the proper setting for effective and accurate communications. (See *Communications,* Chapter 3.)

- **Seat learners close to their source of information.** Distance is a critical factor in human communication. In a lecture situation, the students should be close to the lecturer. In a seminar situation, the group should be physically close (see *Conference Rooms,* Chapter 6). In learning from demonstrations, the student should be close to the demonstration. Amplified voices and projected images are not adequate substitutes for being close.

- **Eliminate intervening cues or signals.** Design the classroom so that nothing extraneous will interfere with communication between the learner and the source of information. Bobbing heads in the front row, extraneous noises, and distracting sounds should be eliminated.

- **Provide ambient conditions that make effective communications possible.**
  1. Provide lighting that will permit learners to see clearly and distinguish details in whatever source of information is being used. In the very common classroom situation where students and teachers interact, this means that the faces of both teachers and students must be illuminated so that expressions and gestures are clearly seen and understood.
  2. Provide the appropriate acoustic conditions so that spoken communications, and the nuances of voice and inflection, are clearly understood. Since part of the benefit of classroom learning is in the opportunity it affords to raise questions and ask for clarification, the acoustic design should ensure that students as well as teachers are clearly heard.
  3. Provide air circulation and room temperatures that will permit both students and teachers to concentrate on the learning process rather than on their discomfort.

- **Concentrate class seating immediately in front of the instructor.** Studies at college and university level uniformly indicate that seating positions in the classroom have a significant bearing on student performance in coursework. Whether students choose their own seats or are assigned seats on some other basis, those who sit in the center of the room, directly in front of the instructor, participate more in class activities, perform better on tests, and receive better grades.

  The distribution of grades according to seating location seems to provide a compelling reason for arranging classroom seating so that students are not only close to the instructor but are also directly in front of the instructor and within the instructor's normal cone of vision. This requirement should be observed in any situation where optimum communication between a speaker and an audience is desired.

TERRITORIALITY

Studies comparing open-plan classrooms in elementary schools with more conventional arrangements are unable to demonstrate any inherent superiority in either form. These same studies do note, however, a marked difference in the behavior of both teachers and students in open-plan arrangements. Because open-plan classrooms usually do not provide complete acoustic control, teachers are inclined to limit themselves voluntarily to quiet activities in deference to their neighbors. Where the open layout does not provide clearly marked boundaries separating "classrooms" from "corridors," students moving through open classroom spaces may be noisy and disruptive.

Classroom seating arrangements can affect communications and grades.

Location of the entrances and the aisles influences the seating pattern of the class.

In the event that an open classroom plan is adopted, certain precautions should be taken to avoid the problems mentioned above.

- **Establish clear territorial boundaries between teaching spaces and other spaces.** The requirements already listed for avoiding distraction during the learning process apply to open-plan schools just as much as any other school. Disruptive traffic through the classroom space interferes with communications.
- **Establish acoustic separation between teaching areas.** If the design of a classroom is such that it inhibits a teacher's selection of class assignments and exercises because of the noise factor, it is functionally deficient.

LECTURE HALLS

The lecture hall can be considered as a bigger-than-average classroom. The principal difference is one of scale, which makes interaction more difficult to achieve. In addition to the recommendations made previously for regular classrooms, the following recommendations help cope with the problem of size.

- **Step or slope the lecture-hall floor and offset adjacent rows of seats.** This will help to eliminate one form of intervening distraction—trying to see through someone else's head. Of equal importance, it makes eye contact between students and instructors almost unavoidable, making it somewhat more difficult for one to ignore the other.
- **Place entrance doors at the lecturer's end of the hall.** When people enter an auditorium or lecture hall from the rear, opposite from the stage or lectern, they tend to select seats along the aisles and favor the rear seats over the front seats. If the room is filled to capacity, or nearly so, this selection process has no appreciable effect. If the hall is only half full, the effect is to present the lecturer with a badly dispersed audience. Putting the entrances close to the stage or lectern, at the "front" of the room, may not achieve a completely compact audience, but it will at least place the bulk of the audience closer to the speaker.

LIBRARIES

While libraries are clearly different from schools, it is equally clear that they are definitely part of the educational system. In the field of independent, self-directed education, it is likely that the public libraries are the primary educational resource for both adults and juveniles.

There are a number of different types of libraries serving different types of users: specialized collections of interest principally to scholars, in-house research libraries operated by corporations and trade associations, film libraries, medical libraries, and music libraries. Two of the most common types, however, are public branch libraries and undergraduate libraries. The recommendations that follow were derived from research in the operations of these two types.

The nature of any library should reflect the needs of its own community and its own group of users. A public library in a neighborhood teeming with school-age children can expect to see a great demand for material that is helpful in completing class assignments. If the local population is elderly, library use will be focused less on the schools and more on the interests of retirees.

In any event, if the principal concern in designing for classroom learning is communications, the principal concern in designing libraries is the special aspect of cue searching called *wayfinding*. This is because so much of library use takes the form of a search for specific information or material. The searcher must quickly learn how to use the system in order to improve the chances of finding what is sought. Wayfinding is not only important within the library; in many cases it is also important in getting to the library.

The wayfinding problems of a library can be identified by following the course of a typical user who, upon finding and entering the library, makes contact with some information source such as a librarian or a card catalog, locates the information, captures it in some form by reading it, copying it, or checking it out, and then exits the library. This is a typical, constantly repeated, sequence that can be expedited if the following suggestions are carried out.

- **Provide library identification signs visible from any approach.** This is just as important for a university library as it is for a public library.
- **Clearly identify the entrance locations.** This is especially important for an urban library that may be surrounded by parking spaces.
- **Place an information center inside the entrance.** Ideally, the first thing one should see upon entering would be a librarian or a librarian's aide. The card catalog, *Reader's Guide to Periodical Literature*, indexes, and other guides to the collection should be placed immediately adjacent to the entrance.
- **Provide "you-are-here" maps at the entrance.** While this kind of assistance is obviously more important in multifloor libraries, it is helpful in any library.
- **Provide identification signs for departments and sections.** Unless there are clear, legible, well-lighted, properly positioned signs, newcomers will have little chance of finding what they want without continual need for assistance.
- **Provide descriptive titles for book sections.** While standard cataloguing systems such as the Dewey and the Library of Congress are highly informative to experienced library users and provide a necessary framework for organizing a library collection, they are not well understood by inexperienced users. Adding plain-language, descriptive titles such as "Biography" or "Biology" not only are helpful to the inexperienced searcher; they improve the chances of serendipitous discoveries that can occur when browsing through the collection is encouraged.
- **Provide seating and writing surfaces close to the point where material is discovered.** Whether these are desks, tables, carrels, or lounge seating, they should be at or within the book shelving area in order to expedite reading or taking notes.

There is no way for a newcomer to tell what this building is.

The only building identification is very hard to find.

The "information" sign should be close to the entrance in any library.

These signs are helpful but would be much better if they were horizontal and oriented properly.

- **Provide copy machines close to the point where material is discovered.**
  Having copy machines readily available not only is a convenience to users; it
  also reduces the temptation to tear the information out of the book.

TERRITORIALITY

Busy libraries are excellent places to observe territorial behavior. Dr. Robert Sommer, a pioneer in the study of environment and behavior, conducted some of his earliest studies in libraries. Since library users periodically return to the bookshelves in search of further information, they need some means of saving their places at the table. In establishing territorial boundaries they have at their disposal not only briefcases, notebooks, jackets, umbrellas, scarves, and purses, but unlimited supplies of books.

The result of this behavior is that typical library furnishings in the form of rectangular tables and movable, armless chairs do not actually accommodate the number of people they were designed for. A table designed for eight users will, because of territorial spread, actually accommodate only five or six. The types of furnishings described below will reduce territorial problems.

- **Provide single seats where possible.** Provide single lounge seats for readers, and single carrels or desks for users who need writing surfaces.
- **Where a common table must be used, provide center dividers to limit territorial expansion.** This approach will only work if the tables are divided into genuinely adequate workspaces.
- **Provide special units for group study.** One territorial problem in busy libraries is the tendency for groups to take over tables for their exclusive use. Group study is not uncommon and should not be ignored. It is best handled by providing separate tables in segregated areas where the noise of conversation will not create a problem.

Territorial spread reduces the number of people who can find a place at the typical library table.

9 HEALTH CARE

One of the most complex building types that architects deal with is the large general hospital. Medical technology is expanding rapidly, requiring more and more highly specialized equipment. As specialized treatment techniques increase, so do needs for specialized personnel, resulting in a more complex building type.

Along with this trend toward higher technology and increased specialization, there is another trend to move certain kinds of care out of the general hospital. Birthing centers are one type of special-care facility that seems to offer some real benefits to patients by allowing the father to assist the mother through the stress of giving birth. Hospices are another: They call for the involvement of families and close friends to sustain the patient through the ordeal of death.

Economics is also having an effect on the nature of hospital operations. Hospital stays are getting shorter. Patients are moving out to Extended-Care Facilities, to Nursing Homes, or even their own homes. Some insurors offer to pay the cost of nursing care at home if the patient prefers the comfort and convenience of the familiar to the aseptic confines of the hospital.

This trend away from the general hospital is due, at least in part, to the fact that it is difficult for the highly specialized staff to deal with a steady flow of patients as though each were a unique individual. Nor are they generally equipped to make it easy for family and friends to lend moral support and assistance to the patients when they need it most. This kind of support is just what the Hospice and the Birthing Center are able to offer. What makes this an especially important element in health care is the fact that in many cases, the mental attitude of the patient is a critical factor in recovery.

In the design of health care facilities it is understandable that the principal focus of concern has been on the needs of the medical and support staffs. They are the ones who are responsible for providing health care and are involved in it full time. The speed, accuracy, and convenience with which they work will affect not only the patient's well-being but also the economics of health care. Patients, on the other hand, are transient: The whole purpose of their care is to restore them to health and discharge them as soon as possible.

While this emphasis is understandable, it does not nurture and exploit a very important resource: the patients' use of their own energies, determination, and self-reliance to deal with their own problems.

The material presented in this chapter is focused largely on the patient and the patient's needs. This is not intended to suggest that the health-care team does not face problems of its own. Few institutions have social structures as complex as the staffs of large hospitals. Thirty or forty categories of specialization may be represented: various physicians and surgical specialists, radiologists, anesthesiologists, pharmacists, laboratory technicians, several categories of nurses, aides, administrators, maintenance workers, and clerical workers. The hospital mix is so rich and varied, and the mission is so intriguing, that it is easy to understand why television is fascinated by the drama of the large general hospital. Unfortunately, there is not enough evidence to permit generalizations about staff relations that would be useful to a designer in actually formulating plans for a hospital. The most constructive course would be to involve the staff directly in developing the design program.

The situation is somewhat different with patients. While they may all differ in nature and suffer from a wide range of afflictions they experience certain problems in common. A building design that is reassuring to them, minimizes the stresses of noise and discomfort, and permits them to retain some feeling of competence and independence can help patients become a functioning part of the health-care system rather than its inert object.

GOING TO THE HOSPITAL

Going to the hospital is a trip viewed with apprehension by patients, family, and friends. The security of the patients' most important possessions, themselves, is put at risk. Already burdened with health problems and apprehensive about their well-being, patients clearly do not need any further stress or uncertainty imposed by their environment. Designers of health-care facilities can do a great deal to eliminate or minimize such sources of stress by the way they arrange the approaches to the building, organize the circulation, and equip the patients' rooms. While the recommendations that follow deal with hospital care, many of these points would apply in any health-care situation.

CUE SEARCHING

Finding one's way to, and into, a large medical center can be a daunting experience. All the problems normal to wayfinding are present: identifying the site, solving the approach, and locating the entrance (see *Cue Searching*, Chapter 3.) If there is confusion or uncertainty about these points, it will vex not only the patients but also their friends and visitors.

- **If the site is large, post signs at all corners.** Some hospital sites are quite large. It helps to know when you are getting closer.
- **Identify the building with well-illuminated signs.** These should be positioned to be visible from every approach. They should not be timid signs. Their purpose is to announce the location of the hospital far and wide.
- **Mark the patient and visitor entrances with pylons and illuminated signs.** Many hospitals, particularly those that have expanded over a period of time, have several entrances serving different purposes. Making the entrance system understandable to patients and visitors in a matter of real concern. The average patient's apprehension about getting to the hospital is nothing compared to the panic felt by someone trying to find the Emergency Entrance in the middle of the night.
- **Provide a highly visible entrance feature.** The purpose of this requirement is to utilize some form of architectural means to emphasize so that it can be seen and identified from a distance.

ENTRANCE AND CIRCULATION

Once patients and their families and friends enter the hospital, their wayfinding problems are by no means ended. Even more important, however, is the fact that they are now within the institution itself and the way in which they are received and treated will affect their attitude about the institution. For a patient to acquire a negative attitude about the hospital upon entering is not helpful for the patient, the hospital, or the doctor who admitted the patient.

It may seem that the hospital has no obligation to the patient's friends and family since they are not the object of health care. This would be an unfortunate assumption. Friends and family are part of the patient's psychological support group and help to sustain the patient's self-assurance and sense of competence.

COMMUNICATIONS

The hospital, as an institution, should attempt to establish channels of communication with patients at the earliest moment. Ideally, the first contact should be made with an introductory phone call before the patient arrives. In any event, the building lobby should be considered the principal point of contact and should communicate an impression of welcome and support.

- **Provide a reception and information center.** There is no information device or system that is nearly as helpful or supportive as a knowledgeable individual to provide information and assistance. Even if it cannot be staffed at all times, there should be an obvious center where the newcomer can turn for information. It should be adjacent to the entrance and clearly visible to anyone entering. A house phone that will always provide access to someone on duty should be provided.

- **Provide a lounge seating area.** Admission procedures are sometimes time consuming. Since many patients are accompanied by friends and family, there should be some place where they could muster and wait as a group.

- **Avoid an austere or institutional mien.** The transition from home to hospital is unsettling. To enter directly into an environment that may be read as remote or disinterested only adds to the stress. There are some parts of a hospital that are unavoidably sterile, technical, and frightening, but the entrance lobby is not one of them. The lobby should be comfortable, the colors should be cheerful, the lights should be bright, and everything in the lobby should be immaculately clean.

    It would be inappropriate to give the lobby a residential character. Patients come to the hospital because they have problems that cannot be taken care of at home. The hospital is a special place and should give patients the feeling that they have put themselves in the hands of an organization that has the knowledge, the experience, and the competence to take care of them. The hospital should create the impression of friendliness and concern but also competence and efficency.

CUE SEARCHING

Given the labyrinthine layout of some hospitals, wayfinding is difficult even for well people, let alone those who are experiencing anxiety about their future. This is particularly true of those hospitals that have grown new wings and annexes over a period of time. Whatever clarity of organization they may have had in the beginning is eventually buried under layers of expansion and change. Helping patients and their friends find their way through these mazes is a serious problem for designers.

- **Develop a hospital plan that can be explained easily to strangers.** This may seem like a pointless admonition, a "Be sure to do a good job" recommendation. It is listed here in the hope that it will be added to the designer's list of mandatory requirements. Hospitals and hospital additions are such complicated planning problems that it is doubtful that the public's wayfinding problems get much attention. They should.

    Determining whether the plan *will* be clear to the public is not difficult. It has been shown that diagrammatic plans of buildings can be used to determine, with considerable accuracy, whether people will have difficulty finding their way in the building itself.

- **Provide a series of "you-are-here" maps.** The first map should be in the entrance lobby as an adjunct to the information center. Others should be located at key points where major pathways cross or where there is some ambiguity that requires clarification.
- **Provide a comprehensive directory.** This should also be located in conjunction with the information center and next to the "you-are-here" map.
- **Provide a comprehensive color, symbol, and sign system to guide people through the hospital.** Starting at the entrance lobby, there should be a continuous system of guidance to lead newcomers to their destinations. Floor, wall, and door colors can be used to identify departments. Color lines on the floor or walls should lead patients to principal destinations. When the elevator doors open on each floor, it should be instantly apparent what the floor number is and what departments are located there. These techniques should be used in conjunction with the "you-are-here" maps previously mentioned.

TERRITORIALITY

Because of the complex social structure of their staffs, hospitals have some complex territorial problems. It is easy to understand how hospital territory would be divided among major departments and their staffs. It is not easy to determine territorial lines when responsibilities overlap. The pharmacy is clearly the preserve of the pharmacist, but when medications are sent to the patient floors to be administered by the nursing staff, do they remain part of pharmacy territory, under pharmacy control, or are they then part of nursing territory and under nursing control?

The territorial questions that concern us are much easier to deal with. There are parts of any hospital that are clearly off limits to the patients, their families and their friends. There are other parts where they have as much right as anyone. This distinction should be made perfectly clear to anyone visiting the hospital.

- **Patients' territory and public territory should be clearly identified.** All those areas that are open to the patients and the public should be clearly identified by color or finish so there is never any question about where they are free to go.

PATIENT ROOMS

Whether a patient's hospital stay is short or long, there are certain aspects of room design that will not only make the stay more comfortable but will also sustain the patient's sense of personal competence and ability to cope with problems. The patient's outlook and determination are important elements in the recovery process. Anything a designer can do to reinforce a patient's sense of dignity and self-worth is a contribution to this process.

One of the most difficult aspects of hospital care is the fact that many people suddenly find themselves sharing a bedroom with one or more strangers. Furthermore, these strangers may be extremely ill, under the influence of powerful medications that induce unusual behavior, suffering from nausea and violent retching, and unable to control their urination and defecation. Even a well-balanced optimist, who is forced to spend the night before surgery with such a roommate, might greet the morning in a depressed mood.

Shared rooms also raise complicated territorial problems. In addition to such obvious problems as sharing the telephone and the television, adjusting the window blinds and ventilation controls can also be sources of friction. An entirely different aspect of the problem is patients' need to personalize their spaces. No matter how short their hospital stay, the patient's room is home for a time. Patients should have some means of displaying cards, flowers, or any other personal mementos they choose to have with them.

There are gregarious people who find shared rooms interesting and some, perhaps, who might be encouraged by the thought that at least they are better off than their roommate. For most adults, however, shared bedrooms are an unusual, and in some ways unattractive, aspect of hospital care.

Whether patients are in private rooms or share rooms with one or more other people, their rooms should encourage them to do as many things for themselves as they can safely do. Self-help of this type benefits the staff to some extent, but the more important purpose is to help patients retain a feeling of independence and competence.

TERRITORIALITY

Hospital rooms have complicated functional requirements having to do with health care operations on behalf of the patient. From the patient's point of view, there are also other considerations that should be included in the design requirements.

- **Provide private rooms for most patients.** While there will be those who would prefer to share a room, particularly if cost is a pressing problem, most patients will avoid stress and frustration if they have their own rooms.
- **Provide soundproof separations between beds.** Whenever shared rooms are provided for reasons of space or economy, provide the means of acoustically isolating each bed. The draw curtain that is traditionally provided between beds for visual privacy is of no value in ensuring acoustic privacy.
- **Position beds so that all have equal access to outside light and ventilation.** Typical shared rooms have one or more beds close to the window and the others close to the corridor. Plans that give all beds equal access to outside light and ventilation minimize some of the problems that are inherent when one bed is favored over another.

    If the room is arranged so that beds face window walls, some special arrangements must be made to control glare.
- **Provide complete facilities for each bed in shared rooms.** The problems with shared rooms can be reduced if each bed has its own set of light and ventilation controls, telephone, TV, and call button.
- **Provide a means for patients to personalize their own spaces.** Whether in shared or private rooms, all patients should have some means of displaying whatever personal mementos have meaning for them.

PERSONAL STATUS

The appearance of the patient's room and the degree to which the patient's needs have been anticipated and taken care of tells the patient something about the hospital's attitude and concern. If an obvious effort has been made to make the room attractive and comfortable, if there are seats for visiting friends, and if there are convenient places for the things people bring with them, the patient will be less likely to feel like another statistic in the hospital computer.

People's sense of personal worth is affected by the degree to which they feel self-reliant and capable of caring for themselves. One of the reasons for being in the hospital, of course, is that during an illness, after surgery, or as a result of treatment, patients are not capable of caring for themselves. As a result, their self-confidence may be at a low point. During the first phase of recovery, it is helpful, and encouraging, if the room is equipped so that patients can do many of the simple, customary things for themselves: sit up, use the toilet, take a shower, shave, and apply cosmetics. The sooner patients are capable of caring for themselves, the sooner they will feel that they are no longer ill.

- **The patient's room should have a pleasant, non-institutional design character.** While the functional requirements of health care come first, once these requirements are satisfied, there is no reason why the hospital room should not be as enjoyable and attractive as possible.
- **Protect the patient from stressful environmental conditions.** The patients field of vision should be free of glare whether they are sitting up or lying down. Noise from mechanical sources such as elevators and air-conditioning systems and the clatter or corridor traffic should be kept out of the room. Most important of all, the sounds made by other patients should be excluded.

The room should be odor free. The smell of disinfectants, medications, and bedpans contributes nothing to the patient's sense of well-being. This means that exhaust systems in the hospital must be worked out carefully.

The patient should have some means of controlling room temperature and air movement.

- **Equip the room for use by the physically impaired.** This is an obvious requirement, since many patients *are* physically impaired. Handrails should be placed along the walls so that patients can help themselves move to the toilet or the closet. Floors throughout the patient room should be nonslip.

The shower and toilet room are dangerous places at home and are no less so in the hospital. They should be equipped with handrails and grab bars to accommodate sure and safe movement. There should be a seat in the shower, since some patients cannot stand for any length of time. A generous shelf should be provided at the washbasin for toilet articles, and a seat should be provided so that the basin can be used while sitting down.

Shared hospital rooms should provide clear territorial boundaries.

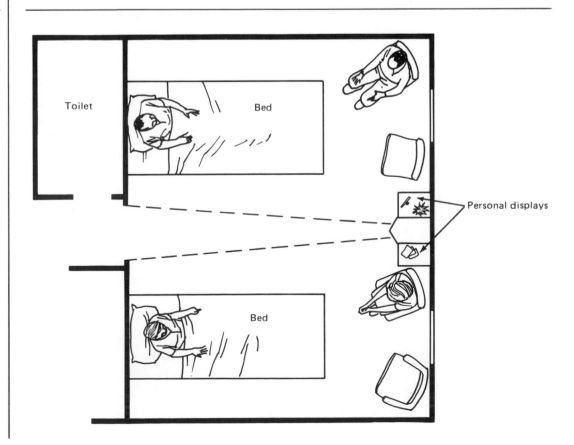

VISITOR FACILITIES

Family and friends are a part of the resources a patient can call on for help in coping with the stress of illness and a strange environment. In that sense, taking care of a patient's visitors is part of taking care of the patient. Other than those special cases where expert medical judgment dictates a "No Visitors" policy, it is generally agreed that visitors play an important part in maintaining patient morale and should be encouraged. One surprising aspect of the visitor situation is that visits drop off sharply during the weekend. A designer who could solve the problem of attracting visitors to the hospital on Saturday and Sunday would make a helpful contribution to the nation's health-care program.

In some aspects of health care, visitors, in the form of family or what human scientists call "significant others," are playing an increasingly important role. This is happening at both ends of life, in birthing centers and in hospices.

Hospital personnel have their own priorities for allocating care, and terminal patients are likely to get more attention from their own visitors and from the semi-professional staff than they are from the MDs and the RNs. In the hospice, a special effort is made to surround the patient with the support of family and friends. Special playrooms may be provided for terminally ill children so that their siblings and other playmates can spend time with them.

Birthing centers also reflect the new understanding of the importance of support from family and friends. Facilities are arranged so that, as far as possible, the father can remain with the mother throughout the childbirth process. Interaction between the family and the newborn infant is encouraged immediately after birth.

The *Joint Position Statement* of the Interprofessional Task Force on Health Care for Women and Children includes a list of recommendations for "Family-Centered Maternity/Newborn Care." It describes birthing rooms, which are a combination of labor and delivery room and are "brightly and attractively decorated and furnished—designed to enhance a home-like atmosphere." This document would be an important resource for designers in the health-care field.

As health care centers move to involve family and friends on behalf of the patient, their needs for specialized spaces such as teaching rooms and family conference rooms will grow. There may well be other kinds of specialized spaces, or modifications of conventional hospital rooms, that will develop as designers grasp the importance of personal support to patients and use that information in a creative way.

The following recommendations deal with conventional visitor requirements. The principles, of course, can be applied in a variety of ways.

CUE SEARCHING

This is as much a problem for visitors as it is for patients. *Provide a comprehensive map and guidance system for visitors.* Visitors have the same problems patients have in navigating hospital corridors. They may not feel that they have the same rights, however, to ask for detailed assistance in finding their way. All of the wayfinding systems spelled out earlier in this chapter are very important to visitors.

PERSONAL STATUS

Visitors' attitudes toward the hospital are affected by the facilities that are provided for them. More important, however, the visitors' feelings that they can be helpful to the patient are affected. It is in the best interest of the patient and the hospital that visitors be made to feel that they are an important resource for the patient and that their visit is appreciated. The hospital's attitude is communicated at a number of different points.

- **Provide a well-equipped general waiting room at or near the major treatment centers.** The waiting room should be near treatment centers so that friends and family can be quickly contacted by the medical staff. It should be furnished with comfortable lounge seating, since the waits are sometimes very long. The furniture should be arranged to accommodate family groups.

  The waiting room should offer some diversions such as television and reading material and should be close to a source of food and beverages.

  Both house phones and outside phones should be provided. The public address system should serve the waiting room.

- **Provide separate waiting parlors for large family groups.** Large family groups that are under great stress may become very emotional. They will be more comfortable if they are moved to a separate room, and the other visitors in the main waiting room will also feel more comfortable.

- **Provide adequate seating in any room where visitors may spend time with patients.** This would certainly be required in the patient's room, and under some systems of care would also be required in the delivery room and during the course of some testing procedures. There should be an allotment of comfortable lounge chairs in each of these spaces, and additional folding chairs should be available if needed.

10 PUBLIC PLACES– INSIDE

Enclosed spaces that are accessible to and used by the public constitute an important design category. All kinds of lobbies and waiting rooms are included in this category. So are bus and airline terminals, spectator sports facilities, public agencies, and governmental offices of all kinds.

The unique importance of these spaces is that they constitute, in many cases, the site of the first contact between an organization or institution and its clients or customers. The nature of that initial contact has much to do with the public's perception of the organization. If the public perceives that its interests and concerns have been carefully considered, they are likely to have a positive reaction to the organization. If they perceive that their interests have been ignored or that they are treated with indifference, they are likely to develop a negative or hostile attitude. Attitudes formed at this point can persist for a long time. Consequently, entrance areas have a unique importance. It is hard to think of any organization that would benefit from antagonizing its clients and customers.

It is normal for a great deal of time and thought to be devoted to the design of public spaces in buildings, and the results are often striking from a design point of view. This does not mean that they necessarily will serve the users well or that they will serve to establish positive feelings about the host organization. Design characteristics that might be intended to convey an image of power and authority could easily be read as intimidating and hostile by someone who needs helpful information rather than grandeur. People entering buildings, particularly first-time users, need to have certain questions answered if they are to accomplish their purposes quickly and efficiently. They will also respond in a positive way to arrangements that contribute to their comfort and convenience.

BUILDING APPROACHES

In Chapter 3, the section dealing with *COMMUNICATIONS* discusses the information that a building should communicate to someone approaching for the first time. Chapter 7 includes additional commentary on this point as it applies to shopping behavior. These same principles apply to the category of buildings discussed here. The first impression made by most buildings, or the first information communicated by most buildings, occurs during the approach to the building when these basic questions are answered:

- What is it?
- What benefit does it offer me?
- How do I get in?
- What is inside?
- How will I be received?

For a detailed discussion of these points, refer to the earlier chapters.

INSIDE THE BUILDING—ENTRANCE AREAS

While we are covering a wide range of building types in this section, ranging from the neighborhood post office to the United Nations Building, there are certain things that are common to all of them. There are also things that are *not* common to all, but those should be readily apparent.

CUE SEARCHING

The first need for anyone entering a building is specific information: "Where do I go?" and "How do I get there?" The range of questions is as varied as the types of buildings. In the Municipal Courts Building it is "Where do I pay my parking fine?" In the post office it is "Where do I pick up my parcel?" In the hospital it is "Where is the Radiology Department?" In the airport it is "Where do I catch the commuter flight to O'Hare?"

The designer of any building, regardless of how modest, attempts to deal with these questions at the entrance area. If this is not done, there are likely to be people wandering through the building, asking for directions from workers who have more important things to do than act as building guides—and who may not have accurate information themselves. As a result a building entrance should provide specific information aids.

- **Provide a receptionist.** Nothing is quite as effective in helping and explaining as another human being. With another human being we are able to look as well as listen, to raise questions and ask for clarifications. The only weakness in this system is if the receptionist is loaded with secondary duties. If there is some pressure to discharge these other duties the receptionist may compensate by ignoring the public.

  A receptionist should be located near the entrance and immediately adjacent to the main stream of traffic.

Reception area at entrance.

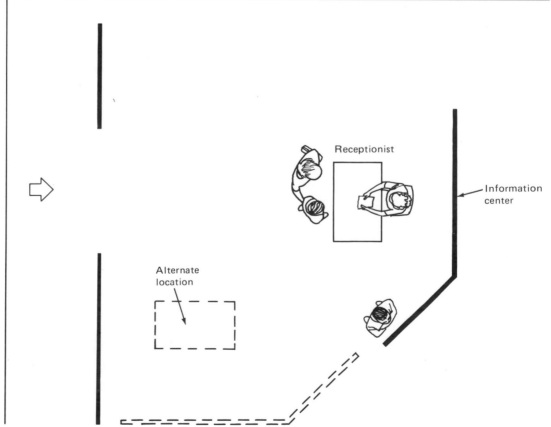

- **Provide an information center.** If it is not possible, or reasonable, to provide a receptionist, an information center should be provided to serve the same purpose. The scale of the information center will vary with the size and nature of the building but all of them should share the following characteristics.

  1. Be located near the building entrance and adjacent to the main stream of traffic. The location should be highly visible.

  2. Contain a well lighted directory with letters of appropriate size and contrast to be easily read.

  3. Provide a "you-are-here" map that is properly oriented and well illuminated.

  4. Allow sufficient space in front of the map and directory so that people can study the information without blocking traffic.

  While an information center is helpful, many people would rather ask questions than read answers. If there is anyone present who appears even slightly knowledgeable, these people will bypass the information center and corner this individual. The result is that people who have other full-time duties, but happen to be located near an entrance, may find themselves spending a good deal of time giving directions. This is a common problem in open-plan establishments such as banks and savings and loans.

- **Provide an intelligible signing system.** This is a more complicated assignment than it seems. A number of conditions must be met to satisfy this requirement.

  1. Signs must have letters of sufficient size, have adequate contrast, and have adequate illumination to be easily read.

  2. Signs must be located within the normal cone of vision and should be at right angles to the line of vision.

  3. Signs should be repeated periodically to reassure newcomers that they are on the right path. It is hard to give precise rules for spacing signs. They should occur whenever a corridor or walkway changes direction and should be repeated at intervals so that people walking at normal speed would get some confirmation that they are on the right path every minute.

- **Tell the story of the building.** This is more important when the building is occupied by one organization or public agency. In such cases some effort should be made to use the entrance area to tell what the organization is and what it does.

PERSONAL STATUS

The term "entrance area" covers a wide range of facilities. The lobby of an office building is one. The lobby of a hotel is another and quite different kind of facility. The "entrance area" in many other buildings, however, is not distinct from the rest of the operating space. Anyone entering a bank to rent a safe deposit box or entering a state office to renew a drivers license, rarely passes through a demarcated entrance area. They enter directly into the space where business is transacted.

In dealing with the way that an individual's sense of personal status is affected by the design of entry areas, a designer must take into account a wide variation in operating conditions. As a result, some of the situations discussed below can be applied to some entry areas but not to others.

An individual entering a building is exposed to certain cues that indicate how much care and thought have been devoted to making it hospitable. Conversely, of course, the cues may indicate how *little* care and thought have been given to that subject. The manner in which these cues are evaluated depends on the individual's needs and the kind of place that is entered. A customer in a discount tire

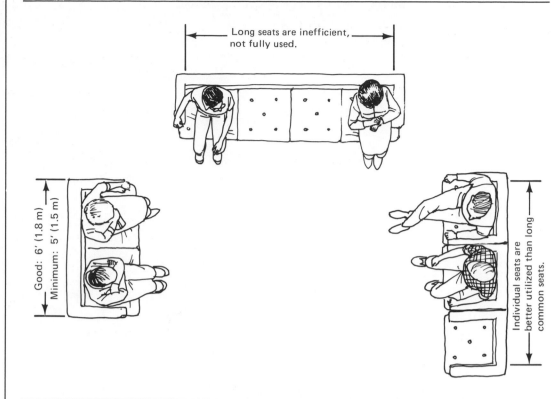

store would be much more tolerant of poor housekeeping than a patient in a dentist's office. In general terms, an entry area should help visitors find their way, make them comfortable, and exhibit an awareness of their special needs. The design should demonstrate that visitors are regarded as important human beings.

- **Accommodate the transition from outside to inside.** Provide a nonskid area where umbrellas may be furled, topcoats or raincoats taken off, and shoes or overshoes wiped off.
- **Provide seating of an appropriate kind and amount.** This would be considered a routine requirement in hotel lobbies but is frequently omitted in other entrance areas.
  1. Provide individual chairs or short couches. Long seats or benches in public places are not efficiently used. After the end positions are occupied, newcomers will generally not take the center seats unless their need to sit down is extreme.
  2. If ganged seats are to be used, provide a distinct separation between arm rests so that territorial boundaries are well defined.
  3. Favor small groups in arranging seating area (see Chapter 3, *Group Membership*). Since a very small percentage of all informal groups exceeds three people, furniture arrangements should favor such groups.
  4. Arrange seating to accommodate conversations. Side by side conversations are not convenient. When given the opportunity, most people will adjust their seating arrangements so that they are at an angle with any companion rather than side-by-side or face-to-face.
- **Provide queueing systems wherever people must wait for service.** The queueing system may be a list maintained by a receptionist, a system frequently seen in restaurants, it may be a "take-a-number" system, or it may be a physical queue. The system should have the following characteristics.

A queueing system that makes it possible to force a queue when the traffic volume requires it. Customers do not have to leave the queue in order to attend to paper work.

1. Provide seating if a lengthy wait may occur. The seating should satisfy the requirements listed above.
2. If a physical queue is planned, provide clear boundaries to discourage queue jumpers. Depending on the good will of the public to form and police an equitable queue is unfair. Some people will be scrupulous in observing the rules of fair play but others will not.
3. Whether people are seated and the queue is in the form of a list, or there is an actual physical queue, provide facilities that people will need to use during their wait or that will make their wait more comfortable. If they must fill out forms while waiting there should be writing surfaces that can be used for this purpose. If they must manage parcels and bundles while waiting, there should be space for them to rest these burdens. If parents with small children will be waiting there should be some activity to occupy the children.

    These conditions should be met whether people are sitting or standing. A standing queue should have writing surfaces and places for parcels for people to use as the line moves along.

■ **Entertain or inform the people who are waiting.** The total number of hours consumed each day by people waiting in some form of queue must be enormous. Any system or technique that can make those waiting hours more enjoyable or more enlightening would relieve a lot of boredom.

WAITING ROOMS

One common destination for people who pass through the entrance area and arrive at the place they are seeking is a waiting room. Waiting rooms range in size from the modest entry in a small professional office to the large but crowded spaces found in some public agencies. Whatever its size and arrangement, the waiting room projects a message about the organization and the way it views its visitors.

It is obvious that the nomenclature used here is very imprecise. When people enter a structure they are clearly at an entrance area. They may also be in a lobby or in a waiting room. Since entry areas have already been discussed, we will assume here that waiting rooms are those spaces set aside by an organization for the use of customers, clients, patrons, applicants, or beneficiaries because the nature of the operation is such that they will almost surely have to spend some time waiting.

Many of the recommendations previously made for entrance areas apply here. There are some special concerns, however, because waiting rooms, for many people, will be associated with some degree of stress or anxiety. This is easy to understand in the case of health care facilities, but it is also a factor for applicants of all kinds, whether they are applying for jobs, credit, scholarships, loans, or welfare benefits.

In view of the potential for stress in a waiting room, the role of the receptionist is especially important. The receptionist occupies the role of gate-keeper, with real or imagined authority to favor one person over another. The design arrangement must minimize this gate-keeper illusion and reassure the waiting public that they will be treated fairly.

■ **Provide space for a receptionist.** An indispensable requirement. Someone must have the responsibility for seeing that people entering the waiting room are greeted and assisted as necessary. The receptionist should be capable of advising them, and having any necessary forms and equipment, so that time spent in the waiting room can be put to good use.

1. Locate the receptionist near the entrance so that everyone entering is greeted, logged in, added to the queue if necessary, and given the proper instructions and forms.
2. Do not enclose or separate the receptionist from the public with glass partitions. This intensifies the gate-keeper effect and makes contacts distant and impersonal.
3. The receptionist should be at the same level as the public.
4. The receptionist is, at that point, the alter ego of the organization and should be able to take care of the needs of the people entering the waiting room without being overburdened with other duties.

■ **Provide seating of the appropriate kind and amount.** See the detailed discussion of this topic in the preceding section.

■ **Provide queueing systems of the proper type.** See the detailed discussion of this topic in the preceding section.

■ **Entertain or inform the waiting public.** There is no reason for people to waste time while waiting. Magazines or brochures explaining the operations of the organization convey the impression that someone considers the people in the waiting room to be important. Aquariums and terrariums are often seen in medical waiting rooms where they serve as a diversion. But there can also be practical, functional displays, Employment offices should obviously post announcements of job opportunities. The purchasing department waiting room should display list of items out for bid for the benefit of waiting vendors. A designer can, without great difficulty, make waiting rooms and waiting time much more interesting and useful than they usually are.

The reception desk is located so that everyone entering is greeted.

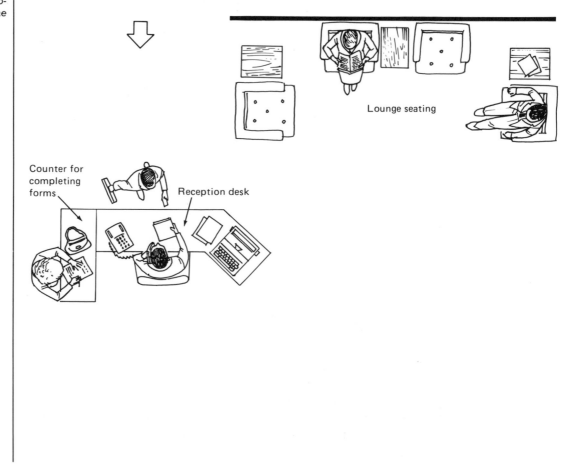

Lounge seating

Counter for completing forms

Reception desk

11 PUBLIC PLACES–OUTSIDE

This category deals with public spaces that are open and available to the public without the payment of admission fees. It obviously includes spaces in the public domain such as parks, plazas, playgrounds, and the grounds of public buildings. To a limited degree it also includes college campuses, some school grounds, and open spaces such as shopping center malls that are privately owned but are available to the public for restricted use.

Open spaces such as these are an important part of the fabric of any community, but they represent only a tiny fraction of the total open space of a city. It is the streets, sidewalks, arcades, alleys, and other unrestricted public spaces that constitute an underutilized community resource of vast proportion.

All of the spaces enumerated above serve some primary practical functions by providing for access, transportation, recreation, and education. In addition they could, and should, serve equally important but not so obvious functions as places for informal social contact and communication.

IN THE PARK

A park functions principally as a public service for the area in which it is situated. It should reflect the special needs of its service area. A park in a downtown business district, used principally during the working week, will have purposes and characteristics that are different from those of a regional park that provides unique recreational opportunities for the residents of a wide area. A neighborhood of single family dwellings, where each family has some private yard space of its own, will have needs different from those of an apartment house neighborhood where the park may provide the only accessible open space for hundreds of families.

The function of most parks is to provide the public with access to experiences that are not normally available to them on their own premises. These experiences fall within the general category of recreation. This may be active recreation, ranging from shuffleboard to basketball, or passive recreation, ranging from bird watching to sunbathing. Regional parks may offer activities as diverse as golf courses, skeet ranges, and model airplane flight centers. Vest-pocket parks may offer nothing more vigorous than chess and checkers. In any event, the accent is on leisure time activities rather than working activities.

Parks also serve other purposes. The fact that people are brought together in pursuit of leisure activities inevitably generates social involvement. Wherever people gather for social purposes they constitute a potential audience. An audience inevitably attracts performers. The result is that if a park attracts many users, their presence generates more activities which in turn attract more users. If park characteristics and facilities are precisely matched to the needs of the service area *at all age levels,* a park can be a dynamic element in any neighborhood.

Apart from the recreational aspects of park use, there are behavioral considerations that have a great deal to do with the amount of use a park receives.

PERSONAL SAFETY

There are some parks in this country that are safe to use at any time of day or night. Unfortunately, this is not universally true. Other parks, particularly in urban centers, are not safe to use after dark and some are subject to violence at any time. Where such hazards exist, adults are reluctant to permit their children to use the park and equally hesitant to use it themselves. What should be a neighborhood asset becomes a neighborhood liability. While no magic formula exists by which a designer can completely eliminate such hazards, there are things that can be done to create situations that are inherently less subject to criminal activity.

- **Design for the needs of the local residents.** This may seem a truism hardly worth mentioning, but it is by far the most effective measure that can be taken to insure a successful, well used park. The more a park is used by all segments of the local population, children and adults, the more they are likely to take the actions necessary to defend it. Unless the local community has strong feelings of "ownership" about their park, and develops political pressure to keep it safe, there is little that anyone can or will do to insure that it is a safe place.
- **Concentrate activities in a limited number of areas.** Concentration of activities results in concentration of people. To some extent there is safety in numbers. The more people there are the more surveillance there is. To the extent that surveillance is a deterrent to crime, concentrating people is helpful in making a park safer.
- **Increase foot traffic through the park.** Increasing traffic is a means of increasing the number of people in the park at any time. There are a number of things that will make a park more attractive to foot traffic simply because it is more interesting than the alternative paths. Food service, event centers, information centers, water displays, floral displays, and playgrounds are all features that make walking through the park more attractive than walking down the street. The most certain way to generate foot traffic, however, is to provide a shortcut to an important destination such as a bus stop, a shopping district, or a school.
- **Maintain good visibility into the park.** One means of improving surveillance of activities in a park is to make it possible to see into the interior from the boundary streets and walks. If the park is to receive any appreciable amount of evening activity, there must be lighting in the activity centers and along the walkways.
- **Provide a protected area for small children.** Even in orderly, safe, park environments, small children can be subject to hazards simply because of their age and size. Play areas for small children should be fenced off so that they will not wander off into street traffic. The fenced area should also protect them from the rough play of older children. Their best protection, however, comes from providing comfortable and convenient seating for their parents or relatives.

FRIENDSHIP FORMATION
GROUP MEMBERSHIP

A park designer needs to know the nature of the park's service area and the recreational needs and preferences of its residents. In providing facilities to accommodate these needs, a designer can also make a contribution to friendship formation in the community.

Any area in a park that generates activity will also generate spectators. If the park provides shuffleboard courts, there will be shuffleboard spectators, commentators, and critics. If the park supports a population of pigeons or water birds there will be bird feeders and bird watchers. If the park accommodates any substantial amount of pedestrian traffic the benches along the walks will be manned by people watchers. If food can be purchased in the park there will be people clustered at the food service area. Activities generate traffic and audiences.

If some of these activities can be clustered, without inhibiting their usefulness, they can form social centers as well as activity centers. This effect is strengthened if the activities are located at a point where important circulation paths intersect. As traffic is drawn to such centers, the chance of meetings between friends and acquaintances increases. If there is a place to stand outside the flow of traffic or, even better, a comfortable place to sit down, a social contact develops. If this kind of event recurs regularly, a social center is born.

Certain conditions should be created to increase friendly contact.

- **Make activity areas visible from the perimeter of the park.** This is simply a matter of making the park's attractions apparent to people passing by.
- **Provide attractive shortcuts through the park.** As stated above, shortcuts generate traffic and increased traffic leads to more social contacts.
- **Arrange walkways to traverse areas of diverse activity.** The more diverse the activities, the greater the possibility that a pedestrian passing by may stop and become a spectator.
- **Provide performance areas along the walk or in the center of the walk.** If the park sponsors performances or encourages spontaneous performances, such locations insure an audience for the performers and added interest for people passing through the park. (see Chapter 6, *Open Assembly*)

A shortcut is one
means of generating
traffic through the
park.

- **Provide seating at park entries and each activity area.** As game courts and
play equipment are essential for active park users, seats and benches are essential equipment for sedentary park users.
- **Arrange seating to facilitate informal social groups.** Much park seating is
relentlessly linear, an arrangement that inhibits group formation because it is
hard for a group to converse if they are seated side by side (see *Communications*,
Chapter 3). Where they can do so, people arrange their seats so that they can
face their conversational partners at an open angle. The best solution is to provide flexible seating so that it can be shifted to suit the needs of the users. If that
is not possible, seating should be arranged at right angles or in open squares so
that groups can form conveniently. Any seating plan must take into account the
fact that some people do not want to be sociable and prefer solitary seating.

Linear seating makes it difficult for social groups to form, unless someone is in a wheelchair.

People adopt a normal arrangement facing each other whenever park seating makes this possible.

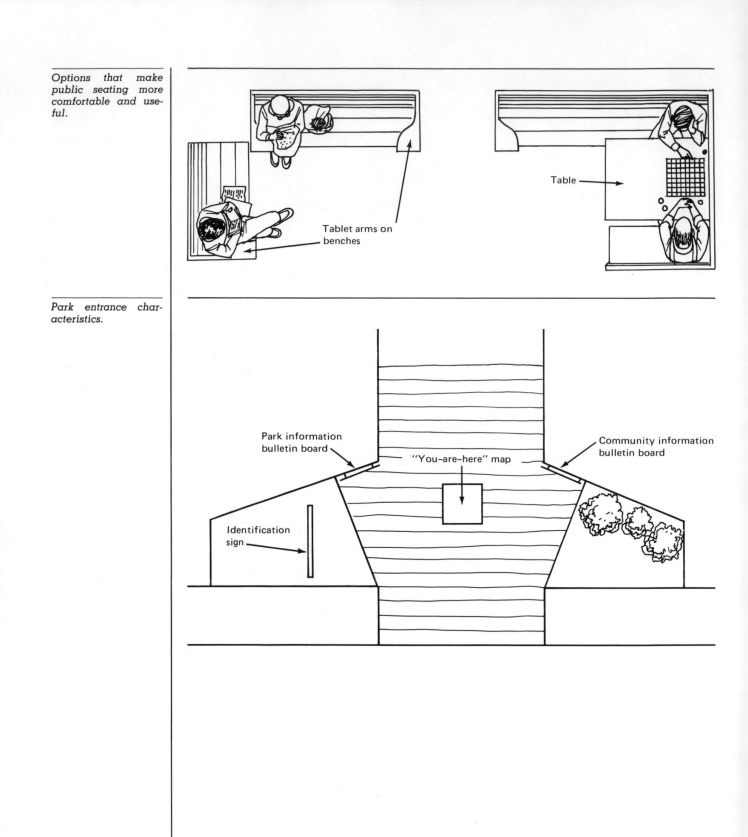

Options that make public seating more comfortable and useful.

Tablet arms on benches

Table

Park entrance characteristics.

Park information bulletin board

"You-are-here" map

Community information bulletin board

Identification sign

COMMUNICATIONS

Like any other institution, parks need to communicate with their potential users if they are to benefit the greatest number of people. It cannot be assumed that "everyone knows" what is in the park. Our national mobility insures that there will always be newcomers in the community who need to be introduced to park resources. The park design will communicate a great deal of information in itself, but there is also a need for the more prosaic but indispensible bulletin board announcing events and programs, telling how to reserve barbecue sites or tennis courts, and establishing the rules of use.

- **Locate park activities so they can be seen by anyone passing by.** An effective way to tell the neighborhood what is going on in the park is to let them see for themselves.
- **Create clearly defined park entrances and develop them as information centers.** Each entrance should have a sign giving the name of the park, the activities provided, and the rules for use. In addition there should be a bulletin board to accommodate changeable announcements about events and seasonal programs.

    If the park is large there should be a "you-are-here" map at each entrance (see *Cue Searching*, Chapter 3).
- **Provide a neighborhood bulletin board at each entrance.** If a park becomes a vital center of neighborhood activity it may also serve as a neighborhood communication center. A bulletin board for public use at each entrance can accommodate announcements of neighborhood organizations and individuals alike.

ON THE STREET

A universal aspect of community life in every age is the public way. This is just as true of nomadic tent cities as it is of the world's great metropolises. Property rights, even transient ones, are of little value unless there is some means of access to the property.

The public way has come to be important in other ways as well. In addition to being the vital artery for the movement of people and goods, it is the setting for the public life of the city. The practice of using the streets for barter and trade, for political rallies and religious revivals, for social gatherings and courtship rites, has dwindled in recent times but has never vanished.

In its original form the street was a pedestrian way. When vehicle traffic made joint use of streets hazardous, pedestrians moved to sidewalks. Vehicles have continued to encroach on the pedestrian space ever since. It is true that increased use of automobiles has reduced the need for sidewalks in some areas. There are other areas, however, where the need for hazard-free pedestrian traffic has reversed this trend. Heavy truck traffic has been removed from many city streets and, in some shopping districts, the streets have been closed to vehicular traffic completely. Such downtown malls, and the ubiquitous suburban shopping mall, return the street to something like its original role as a setting for the public life of the community. They demonstrate that people are still able to walk and will do so if it is worth their while.

Street and sidewalk needs differ in different districts of the city. The features required in a downtown business district, with heavy pedestrian traffic, differ from those that are required in an apartment district. The sidewalks in a neighborhood of single family dwellings, if any, serve yet another set of requirements. The fundamental difference between these examples relates to the presence of children. If there are children living in the district, sidewalks are an important asset for them.

Traffic barriers protect, and reassure, pedestrians on the sidewalk.

Surface texture on the sidewalks can be used to provide a tactile warning to pedestrians.

The following discussion deals with the social and behavioral aspects of the public way rather than its function as a traffic artery.

PERSONAL SAFETY

While people can injure themselves in many ways on streets and sidewalks, by slipping on icy pavement for instance or colliding with a mailbox, the principal hazard is the close proximity of moving vehicles. Anything that will keep the two streams of vehicular and pedestrian traffic separated will improve the safety of the streets for pedestrians.

- **Deploy barriers between cars and pedestrians.** Continuous barriers are best. If they are not possible, deploy the sidewalk furnishings, lamp posts, mailboxes, fire hydrants and traffic standards along the curb to provide an intermittent barricade. These can be annoying to motorists who park at the curb but if they are positioned properly they can create a protected sidewalk without interfering seriously with parking.
- **Provide frequent controlled crossings.** These are a nuisance to motorists and a blessing to pedestrians. There is not much room for compromise here. If there are not frequent controlled crossings, pedestrians are tempted to cross wherever they choose in spite of the hazard.
- **Locate traffic signals for pedestrian use.** Traffic signals are sometimes located as though they were exclusively for the control of automobile traffic. If they are also to safeguard pedestrians they must be positioned so that they are equally visible from the sidewalk.
- **Use surface textures to warn pedestrians of traffic hazards.** Pedestrians who are involved in conversation may be relatively oblivious to the hazards of their surroundings. If they have been moving along a protected sidewalk they should be warned that they are approaching an exposed corner. One effective way to alert them to change is to alter the sidewalk texture drastically at the corner and along the curb.

CUE SEARCHING

In any part of a community where significant numbers of visitors or newcomers may be found, the streets should provide the kind of information that they need to navigate safely and effectively in a strange milieu. This situation is most likely to be found in major business or commercial districts. The visitors there are not necessarily from out of town. They may be suburbanites who do not get into town frequently enough to know their way around.

- **Provide "you-are-here" signs at principal corners.** Properly designed and located, these can be a real boon to city visitors.
- **Provide transit maps and schedules at transit stops.** Another boon for city visitors. People who use a transit system every day have no idea how confusing it can be to a newcomer.
- **Provide directional signs for important locations or events.** All information signs would be more effective if they were concentrated in a coordinated display at a consistent, predictable location at each intersection.

COMMUNICATIONS

People moving along busy downtown sidewalks appear to be rather oblivious to their surroundings. That is why tourists and visitors are so easily spotted in such crowds. They move in a more uncertain manner, visually exploring their surroundings. These different modes of movement are both normal. In a new environment people tend to move in an exploratory mode, proceeding slowly and scanning the environment carefully. In familiar surroundings they move in an habitual mode, moving with confidence and paying little heed to surroundings.

This would seem to indicate that tourists and newcomers are the only ones who are actively searching for cues and are interested in new information but this is not correct. Anyone on the sidewalk, even those who appear to be moving in a trance, will quickly respond to interesting information and events. In spite of the movement and confusion, the sidewalk can be a good place for certain kinds of communications.

- **Provide a window shopping lane.** Pedestrian traffic can also be quickly diverted by merchandise displays. In districts where the sidewalk frontage is occupied by retail shops, a narrow lane or series of alcoves should be provided so

Useful information, located where it is needed.

that pedestrians can stop and window shop outside the stream of traffic. These may be on the public right-of-way or an easement over the commercial frontage. The window shopping lane should be a different texture and color.

- **Provide a protected area for news vending.** Protected in this sense means out of the line of traffic. People on the sidewalk seem to have a boundless appetite for news. Even the most purposeful executive can be diverted by a headline. There should be some place to stand while scanning a headline without being trampled by other pedestrians or creating a sidewalk bottleneck.
- **Provide signboards for community communications.** The sidewalks offer an excellent opportunity for a community to communicate with its citizens. Community programs and coming events of general interest can be publicized effectively in this manner.

A window shopping lane eases sidewalk congestion.

FRIENDSHIP FORMATION

Sidewalks have not completely lost their function as a place for social contact. The big city practice of taking an office building elevator down to a basement garage, driving a few blocks to another basement garage, and taking an elevator up to a roof top restaurant or luncheon club does reduce the likelihood of chance encounters with friends on the sidewalk. There are some limits, however, to the sensible use of automobiles, so that sidewalks will never be completely abandoned. If they were better designed, they might attract more people out of their cars.

An essential element of friendship formation is repeated contact. Acquaintances encountered on the sidewalk might become friends but only if the contact moves beyond perfunctory greetings. Certain conditions are necessary before this is likely to happen.

The first step in social contact is almost always eye contact. Once eye contact is made with someone you know, it would generally be considered rude not to make some further acknowledgement of the meeting. Such an acknowledgement can be expanded if there is a place for it and if both parties are willing.

- **Provide a place for people to stand outside the stream of traffic.** This does not require much space. The eddy in pedestrian traffic caused by a lamp post or mailbox is enough space for two people to converse.
- **Provide a place for people to sit outside the stream of traffic.** This requires more space than standing room. Sidewalk seating is rather rare in urban business districts but it can be a valuable addition to the street scene. Not only does it offer a place for friendly discourse and impromptu business deals, it also offers weary shoppers an opportunity to contemplate their feet.
- **Provide a place for children to play.** Children's needs for socializing and play space are an important consideration in street and sidewalk. Children also need to make friends and the process requires the same continuing contact that is required for adult friendship formation. Blocked streets and true cul-de-sacs provide a reasonable opportunity for street play. Streets that carry significant amounts of through traffic require some other solution. Other than occasional parks and playgrounds, the only other options for children's play are the public sidewalks and private lawns. If sidewalks in residential districts could provide wider areas for small groups of children to congregate it would greatly improve children's play options.

The recommendations made here for making sidewalks more useful and appealing, whether in public ways or in shopping malls, would undoubtedly require more space than is usually assigned to this purpose. The importance of sidewalks in the public life of the city clearly justifies an additional commitment of both space and money.

ANNOTATED BIBLIOGRAPHY

The conclusions presented in this book are based on research information drawn from many sources. Much of it stems from research activities undertaken by the author, in collaboration with Dr. Thomas Lasswell, in connection with various architectural design projects. More of it, however, comes from the *Proceedings* of the Environmental Design Research Association, from periodicals such as *Environment and Behavior*, and from privately circulated papers. Many books were also consulted, ranging in subject matter from urban anthropology to street behavior.

Many of these sources would be difficult for most readers to obtain. The following list of books has been selected because they are especially relevant to the design field and should be available in many research libraries.

Alexander, Christopher. *Notes on the Synthesis of Form*. Cambridge, Mass.: Harvard University Press, 1964.
An important book on design theory. Discusses the process of generating architectural forms from social, psychological, and functional needs.

Appleyard, Donald. *Livable Streets*. Berkeley: University of California Press, 1980.
Discusses the impact of traffic on the neighborhood and explores planning options for making the streets more livable.

Berelson, B., and Steiner, G. *Human Behavior*. New York: Harcourt, Brace & World, 1964.
An encyclopedic compendium of information about human behavior, covering such topics as perceiving, learning, motivation, communications, and attitudes.

Canter, David. *Fires and Human Behavior*. New York: John Wiley & Sons, 1980.
A collection of articles and essays on fire hazards in buildings and human behavior in actual fires.

Cooper, Clare. *Easter Hill Village*. New York: Free Press, 1975.
A comprehensive post-occupancy evaluation of a public housing project. Examines the use of space outside and inside, the children, and residents' reactions to design features.

Deasy, C. M. *Design for Human Affairs*. Cambridge, Mass.: Schenkman Publishing Co., 1974.
Demonstrates the importance of using information and procedures from the human sciences in the design process with actual examples from the author's own architectural practice.

Farbstein, Jay, and Kantrowitz, Min. *People in Places*. Englewood Cliffs, N.J.: Prentice-Hall, 1978.
Discusses how people relate to the places they use and enjoy.

Hall, Edward T. *The Hidden Dimension*. New York: Doubleday & Co., 1966.
An anthropologist looks at the human response to space and how our sense of personal space is determined by culture.

Hall, Edward T. *The Silent Language*. New York: Doubleday & Co., 1959.
Discusses how our social mannerisms, which are dictated by culture, serve as a form of communication.

Harrigan, John, and Harrigan, Janet. *Human Factors Programs for Architects, Interior Designers, and Clients.* San Luis Obispo, Cal.: Meyer, Merriam & Associates, 1976.
Deals with the value of human factors studies in solving architectural design problems. Describes research methods such as observations, questionnaires, interviews, and activity analysis.

Lifchez, Raymond; Williams, Dennis; Yip, Chris; Larson, Michael; and Taylor, Joanna. *Getting There.* Sacramento: California Department of Rehabilitation, 1979.
Examines problems of access for handicapped people. Defines means of identifying such problems and developing effective solutions.

Manning, Peter. *Office Design: A Study of Environment.* Liverpool: University of Liverpool, 1965.
An unusually thorough post-occupancy design study of the headquarters building of a large insurance society conducted by the Pilkington Research Unit of the University of Liverpool.

Marans, Robert, and Spreckelmeyer, Kent. *Evaluating Built Environments: A Behavioral Approach.* Ann Arbor: Institute for Social Research, University of Michigan, 1981.
A comprehensive post-occupancy evaluation of the Federal Office Building in Ann Arbor, Michigan, based on surveys of the building occupants and the using public.

Newman, Oscar. *Defensible Space.* New York: Macmillan Publishing Co., 1973.
A study of crime problems in urban housing, especially public housing, and the effect of building design on the safety of the occupants. An important source for anyone involved in the design of urban housing.

Panero, Julius, and Zelnick, Martin. *Human Dimensions and Interior Space.* New York: Whitney Library of Design, 1979.
A collection of anthropometric data applied to a wide variety of architectural settings. Makes recommendations in a form easily used by designers.

Proshansky, Harold M.; Ittelson, William H.; Rivlin, Leanne G. *Environmental Psychology.* New York: Holt, Rinehart & Winston, 1970.
A collection of essays on various aspects of behavior and environment: theory, research methods, individual needs, and environmental planning applications.

Sommer, Robert. *Design Awareness.* San Francisco: Rinehart Press, 1972.
An early work by one of the pioneers in the field of environment and behavior. Discusses the need people feel to participate in the decisions that affect their lives and their environment. Proposes an evaluation system for buildings and parks and the development of a data bank for future use.

Sommer, Robert. *Personal Space: The Behavioral Basis of Design.* Englewood Cliffs, N.J.: Prentice-Hall, 1969.
A classic in the field.

Sommer, Robert. *Social Design.* Englewood Cliffs, N.J.: Prentice-Hall, 1983.
A discussion of the process by which behavioral information can be obtained and used in the architectural design process by a psychologist who has served as a consultant to both architectural firms and public agencies.

Steele, Fred I. *Physical Settings and Organizational Development.* Reading, Mass.: Addison-Wesley Publishing Co., 1973.
Focuses on how physical surroundings influence the effectiveness of an organization. Considers such factors as security, social contact, tasks, and symbolism.

Van der Ryn, Sim, and Silverstein, Murray. *Dorms at Berkeley.* Berkeley: Center for Planning and Development Research, University of California, 1967.
A study of high-rise dormitories on the Berkeley campus. Observations, interviews, and activity logs were used to determine how the facilities were actually used in contrast to the program assumptions.

Zeisel, John, and Griffin, Mary. *Charlesview Housing.* Cambridge, Mass.: Harvard University School of Design, 1975.
A study of public housing in Boston using observations and interviews to compare the actual building use with the designer's assumptions about its use.

INDEX

Edited by Stephen Kliment and Susan Davis
Designed by Areta Buk
Drafting by Vantage Art
Text set in 11-point Baskerville